The Executive's Guide
to
Management Accounting
and
Control Systems

WILLIAM ROTCH
BRANDT R. ALLEN
C. RAY SMITH
University of Virginia
Colgate Darden Graduate School of Business Administration

1982

Dame Publications, Inc.
P.O. Box 35556
Houston, Texas 77035

© DAME PUBLICATIONS, INC. 1982

ISBN 0-931920-35-3
Library of Congress Catalog Card No. 81-70861
Printed in the United States of America

The Executive's Guide
to
Management Accounting
and
Control Systems

Preface

This book is designed for managers or people who expect to be in managerial positions. Thus, it provides the basis for what a manager needs to know about accounting and control systems. It is a short book and does not try to include everything that could be important. Its purpose is to provide a foundation on which to build.

The book's title describes its subject matter. Management accounting is not a subject separate from management control but rather should be regarded as one of a number of components of management control systems. The early part of the book concerns internal accounting systems designed to help managers run an enterprise. Later chapters broaden the focus to include other aspects of control systems, such as capital budgeting and measures of profitability and performance.

The book is designed for use in a number of settings. We have used it in the second semester of our first year MBA Accounting course. In our case students will have had a semester of Financial Accounting. However, that prior study is not necessary if students review the book's two Appendices, one on the basic accounting process and one on understanding financial statements.

The book has also been used successfully in a variety of executive programs as well as in introductory undergraduate courses. Most instructors use cases along with the text to amplify the ideas and techniques and to provide the application experience which tests and confirms one's understanding of the subject matter.

ORGANIZATION OF THE BOOK

Parts One and Two are concerned with the development and use of cost information. Such information is important in a number of managerial functions: planning, pricing, choosing among alternative actions, and review of actual performance. Effective use of cost information in these functions relies on knowledge of how it was developed and these chapters are designed to provide the essential elements of that knowledge.

Part Three examines the capital expenditure decision. Since these decisions affect operations for years into the future careful analysis is needed including the time value of money.

Part Four expands the viewpoint taken thus far and discusses the system with which management controls and directs an enterprise. A management control system includes the cost systems discussed in Parts One and Two as well as the capital expenditure system of Part Three, and combines these systems into a comprehensive planning and review scheme which is designed to help the enterprise achieve its goals.

Chapter 10 explores briefly the impact of inflation on management decisions. The emphasis here is not so much on the financial reporting issues which are indeed critical and complex, but more on the meaning to those who manage an enterprise. The impact can be confusing and the purpose here is to provide a basic understanding on which further analysis can build.

Appendix A on Basic Accounting Processes and Appendix B on Understanding Financial Statements are included to provide a very basic knowledge of these two aspects of financial accounting.

ACKNOWLEDGEMENTS

From use of this material for over eight years in several schools of business and many executive programs we have received numerous suggestions for change and clarification. In this second edition, as well as in the first, we have followed many of these in order to improve the book where possible.

For this second edition we are indebted to Ramona Wood who typed the manuscript with accuracy and patience making the project an easier one for us.

William Rotch
Brandt R. Allen
C. Ray Smith

Contents

part one

costs for use in management decisions

1

Defining the Uses for Cost Information

How much does it cost?

How much does it cost to make a television set, a ton of paper, a submarine, a fast food hamburger or this book? Or how much does it cost to carry a letter from Seattle to Chicago, to run a bank's installment loan department, or to provide a kilowatt of electricity at 2:00 p.m. on a hot day in New York?

How much does it cost now; how much will it cost next year? Or how much would it cost if activity went up 30% or if volume dropped by 20%?

Fair questions. They are asked every day. They may sound simple, but they are usually complex, or at least difficult to answer precisely. Sometimes there will be two or three right answers. For example, suppose an automobile assembly plant is at one shift capacity and plans to use overtime to increase volume from 500 to 600 cars a day. The manufacturing cost per car at 600 per day will not be the same as it has been at 500 per day. With such an increase, higher unit labor costs are likely to result from overtime; but since no additional facilities would be needed, depreciation and capital costs per car would be lower. The cost of each additional car would depend on how the increases and decreases balanced out. The cost per car, therefore, will be one amount for the first 500 cars but a different amount for the incremental 100 cars a day. There will be no single correct figure for the cost of a car. The correct figure will depend on the specific circumstances and the intended use of the information.

WHERE MANAGERS USE COST INFORMATION

Since the appropriate cost figure depends on how it is used, let us start by examining the main activities in which cost data play a part. Each of these activities is a part of the overall business picture and all are important: planning, pricing, product or service profitability, process efficiency and manpower performance.

Planning

A firm's planning function, whether long- or short-range, relies on cost information. For example, plans for marketing strategy need data on cost-volume relationships. Development of facilities and evaluation of capital projects require projections of costs and savings; even financial forecasting uses cost estimates. It must be remembered, of course, that costs of past activities will not necessarily apply to the future and when past costs are used in planning they must be adjusted to reflect estimates of future conditions.

Pricing

Part of the input to a pricing decision will be the cost of the product or service. If a company produces only one product, the total cost of the product will be fairly easy to obtain. However, most companies produce more than one product and some of the costs incurred are common to several or to them all. Allocating the common costs is therefore a problem. Furthermore, changes in selling prices usually influence the number of units sold and consequently the number produced. Different levels of production will in turn mean different costs per unit produced because, while some production costs vary with volume, others remain relatively fixed. Computing unit costs at different levels of production will therefore require knowledge of which costs vary with volume and to what extent.

Pricing decisions in service businesses are also influenced by costs. However, for several reasons development of useful cost information is more difficult in service businesses. One reason is the low consistency or homogeneity of service business output. Though the content of some services may be fairly consistent and precisely described (e.g., a hamburger), other services can vary greatly (e.g., hospital treatments or bank loans). Thus, the work that goes into the service "product" can be difficult to define and therefore the cost of a service is often difficult to measure.

Another difficulty in costing services arises from the frequently high proportion of indirect and common costs. In the restaurant business one hears that food costs should be no more than 40% of the selling price. The other costs such as for waitresses, cooks and rent are all indirect to a menu item. Computer service bureaus may have over 90% indirect costs. Nevertheless, service businesses need good cost information as much as any other business does. Unless management has some idea of how its costs relate to its prices, it may find itself in the unexpected philanthropic process of an orderly donation of its assets to its customers.

Product or Service Profitability

Having developed costs to help set prices, management will also want cost information to help measure the profitability of products or groups of products. Here the actual costs of the work done and items sold will be important. Also on occasion estimates of future costs will be needed to evaluate the profitability of alternative product mixes or of new products not yet offered.

Process Efficiency

Just as product costs help in decisions affecting a product, process costs are needed to evaluate process efficiency or proposed changes to a process. For example, one multistage machine may replace several single stage machines. The cost information needed to evaluate that change is the cost of that process, which may be only a small part of the total cost for a variety of products. Or consider a bank which offers a collection of services, each of which is often made up of several processes. Evaluating the efficiency of these processes requires focusing on the intermediate steps rather than on the service provided at the end.

Manpower Performance

Evaluating the performance of individuals or groups of people is important, and to do this management needs to be able to measure their activity in terms of cost and output. Frequently standards are established in terms of budgets or standard cost per unit, and actual performance is measured against these standards.

THE VALUE OF COST INFORMATION

Theoretically, the money and effort required to develop cost information should always be balanced against the value of the data produced. As a practical matter this is hard to do precisely, primarily because the "value" of data is hard to pin down. However, one test of usefulness may on occasion be quite revealing. That test is whether the cost information does in fact influence anyone's behavior. Commercial enterprises usually cannot afford the luxury of developing data of interest only to historians, but it is surprising how often data are produced because someone once thought they might be interesting.

THE NEXT TWO CHAPTERS

The next two chapters discuss: first, the general organization of cost data; and then the process of selecting and computing costs that are relevant to particular decisions.

Chapter 2 provides the basic framework for organizing the cost information. It describes how costs are assembled so that management can have a product cost for inventory, the cost of goods or services sold or the cost of running a department. The hardest part about this process is allocating common costs, or costs that are not clearly and directly related to a product or department. These are costs such as the plant manager's salary, electricity and fuel, the quality control department, plant maintenance or production engineering. If all these costs are to be distributed to products, some allocation method is needed; yet for these common costs, no allocation method is demonstrably "accurate" or "correct." Since large amounts of costs are often involved, much time is spent analyzing and choosing methods. The chapter will elaborate on this thorny accounting problem.

Chapter 3 examines ways in which the methods of computing costs must be related to their use for the decision at hand. It builds on the notion that there is no single cost figure for a product which applies to all kinds of decisions. This chapter explains why it is true that in order to obtain the right cost, one must consider both the object or process being costed and the purpose for which the cost is being computed.

2

Organizing the Cost Information

An enterprise incurs many different kinds of costs: for people, material used, electricity, supplies, repairs, new machinery, commissions, and of course for accountants. These costs need to be organized before they can be used in planning and controlling the enterprise. Sometimes costs need to be organized and related to organizational units; sometimes the same costs need to be related to products or services. In this chapter we will discuss how these relationships are determined and point out ways in which the method used may affect the usefulness of the resulting cost information.

CLASSIFICATION OF COSTS

The development of useful cost information starts with the raw data of day by day cost incurrence. The great variety of costs must be organized, put into categories, and summarized so that the results can be used in management decisions.

Costs are usually classified in three basic ways:

a. *by function*, e.g., material, labor, advertising, rent, etc.
b. *by organizational unit*, e.g., machining department, shipping department, quality control section, president's office, etc.
c. *by product or service*, i.e., the output of the organization or that which is sold to customers.

7

Some companies, primarily small ones, classify costs only by functional type. Where there is no inventory, that is the only classification required by the Internal Revenue Service. Some organizations, particularly service, government and non-profit organizations, use only functional and organizational. They set up budgets by department and collect costs in the same departmental groupings. Other firms use only the functional and product categories. Job shops, for example, may collect costs of material, labor and overhead by job, not attempting to relate these costs to departments. However, most larger companies use all three methods so that they have data by function, by department and by product or service.

Chart of Accounts

The way in which an organization categorizes its costs is reflected in its "chart of accounts," which is a numbering scheme that codes costs by their category. For example, a small job shop might use the following system.

Chart of Accounts

Functional	Dept.	Subclass	Job	
100				Payroll
	110			Payroll in department 1
		111		Full time hourly payroll
		112		Part time hourly payroll
		etc.		
200				Material
		201		Material in raw material inventory, type 1
		202		Material in raw material inventory, type 2
	212			Type 2 inventory charged to dept. 1
		etc.		
300				Overhead
		301		Utilities
		302		Rent
	etc.			
			111-A	Full time hourly payroll charged to job A

In this scheme the first digit designates the basic function; the second digit the organizational unit incurring the cost; the third, a sub-classification; the letter designates the job that the cost applies to.

Obviously the system illustrated here is very limited. More elaborate charts of accounts may have as many as 16 digits in an account number, allowing much greater detail and more ways to summarize costs.

In the remainder of this chapter we will examine in more detail each of the three basic ways of classifying costs. Since all organizations use functional categories, we will review these first. Then we will consider classification of costs by organizational unit, including the process of allocating costs that are common to several units. In the last section we will examine how the costs of products and services are developed.

USING FUNCTIONAL COST CATEGORIES

Most manufacturing companies put costs in the following categories:

Manufacturing costs, which are applied to inventory and cost of goods sold. They are sometimes called "costs incurred under the factory roof." Manufacturing costs are made up of:

> Direct Material
> Direct Labor
> Manufacturing Overhead

Selling expenses, including advertising, commissions and salaries of people handling the marketing function. These costs are not added to inventory, but are expensed in the period in which they are incurred.

General administrative expenses, which include top management, staff salaries, office expenses and all other expenses not directly related to production. These costs are expensed each period.

A merchandising firm would categorize its costs somewhat differently. The following categories are generally used:

Cost of merchandise, including inward transportation.

Direct operating expenses, including the cost of operating retail or wholesale outlets, sales salaries and commissions, markdowns, etc.

General administrative expenses, including all other expenses.

A service operation generally has little or no inventory and consequently would normally include two main categories.

Direct operating expenses for the costs of activities directly related to providing the service.

General administrative expenses for all other expenses.

Within these general categories many accounts will provide much more detail. How much detail there should be depends on a cost benefit trade-off. For example, is "office supplies" detailed enough, or should paper, pencils, typewriter ribbons all have separate accounts? Or perhaps paper supplies should be broken down further, separating printed letter paper from blank copying paper. Since additional breakdown raises the cost of processing accounts, a clear benefit should be foreseen for greater detail.

Functional cost categories are a natural first stage in gathering costs. Though these categories alone do not usually provide sufficient cost information for management's decisions, they are often useful in controlling costs. It helps to know how much was spent on telephone service or lubricating oil. Furthermore, the categories, if detailed enough, will contain homogeneous expenses that can be handled as a group when managers plan ahead, or that can be expected to vary predictably with changes in volume.

RELATING COSTS TO ORGANIZATIONAL UNITS

There are two basic purposes for relating costs to organizational units.

For control purposes. Accounting systems do not control costs, people do. Ideally all costs of an enterprise should be related to the person who can be held responsible. Relating costs to an organizational unit is one way of doing this. For example, if Harry Schroeder is in charge of the plating department, then Harry should be responsible for the costs incurred by the plating department. Costs of a variety of functional types would be incurred there: materials, supplies, labor, etc.

For the purposes of developing products costs. A product may pass through several departments and management must be able to apply department costs to the various products that a department works on. Thus, before we can tell how much it costs to plate 1,000 cambolts we must know how much it costs to operate the plating department. That cost, together with the time required to plate the cambolts, will give us a cost per cambolt.

Distributing costs to organizational units is easy for some costs but hard for others. Labor and materials costs are usually easy because they are *directly* incurred by a department. Others, such as the cost of heat, industrial engineering or production supervision are *indirect* and have to be allocated in some logical way. Some costs may be direct, but because they are impractical to measure are treated like indirect costs and allocated. For example, one could use a meter to measure the electricity used by each department. However, except in rare cases of high consumption, the cost of measuring each department is too high to be practical and instead the total electricity cost for the plant is allocated to the various departments.

Thus, there are two reasons for collecting costs by department: for control purposes and for product costing. More will be said in the next section about product costing and Part Four of this book discusses designing and implementing management control systems. Before going on, however, a few observations about cost control are in order here.

ACCOUNTABILITY

Though it is important that someone be responsible for all costs, it is not fair to make a department manager accountable for all the costs charged to his or her department. For example, Harry Schroeder does not control all of the costs in his plating department. He has little control over heat, rent, production supervision and most other indirect costs.

Who, then, should be held accountable? It will have to be someone further up in the organization, possibly the plant manager himself. In theory, the person who has most control over the costs should be the one held accountable. In practice, control is often less than complete. If the weather outside determines how much heat is needed, no one inside has complete control. In practice we are really concerned with influence. Whoever has the most influence should be the accountable person.

Thus, relating costs to organizational units does not solve all the problems of cost control. It is important to consider how much control or influence the unit manager has over the costs assigned to his or her unit. However, unless costs are assigned to people, it will be difficult to assign responsibility.

Organizing costs by area of responsibility is therefore a part of the management control process.

DEVELOPING PRODUCT OR SERVICE COSTS

If the purpose of a firm is to sell a product or provide a service at a profit (or, in the case of not-for-profit organizations, at breakeven), then many decisions depend on the cost of that product or service. Developing these costs is a process of relating input costs to output products or services. We shall start with product costing methods in manufacturing situations which are more complex and comprehensive than costing procedures in merchandising or service operations. Most of the costing procedures used in merchandising and service businesses are found in manufacturing businesses.

Generally accepted accounting principles say that the product costs used to put a value on inventories or cost of goods sold, should be manufacturing costs, or as we have said, costs under the factory roof. However, for some purposes, such as for a government contract, all or substantially all costs may be allocated. In these instances the non-manufacturing costs, such as administrative and selling costs, are allocated to products in much the same way that manufacturing overhead is allocated. Though this total allocation is sometimes appropriate, we shall confine our discussion to the more common situation in which only manufacturing costs are allocated to products.

Direct Product Costs

Costs can be either direct or indirect. In the previous discussion we were concerned with whether costs were direct or indirect to an organizational unit such as a department. Now we are concerned with whether costs are direct or indirect to a product or service. The same costs may be direct to a department but indirect to a product. Such would be the case with material handlers who work in just one department but handle all the products which pass through the department.

It is important to distinguish direct from indirect costs because they are treated differently in computing product costs. The direct cost of a product is usually easy to compute. For example, the amount of material or hours of labor that go into each item can be derived from specifications or time studies. The indirect costs, however, are much more trouble because they are shared by a number of products and hence must be allocated. It might also be noted that the indirect costs have generally increased in proportion to the total as manufacturing processes have become more complex and as more people work on the production system and fewer on the production line.

Separating Direct and Indirect Labor Costs

Methods of distinguishing direct from indirect labor costs vary. Some labor expenses are clearly direct to a product, such as costs for machine operators and assemblers. Other labor expenses are clearly indirect, such as costs for production schedulers, industrial engineers, and plant managers. In between are costs for people like material handlers, who could be considered direct if they clocked the time they spent moving each product around the plant. This timekeeping is usually more effort than the information is worth; therefore, labor costs such as these are considered indirect and are allocated to products along with other indirect labor costs. Thus, the separation of direct from indirect labor costs depends first on whether the costs can be traced to specific products and secondly on whether the cost of the required bookkeeping warrants the effort.

Along with an employee's base wage go fringe benefits such as vacation and holiday pay, pension costs, social security, and perhaps insurance premiums. These increments can easily amount to 20-30% of base pay. Also, if the employee earns them, there may be overtime pay, shift premiums, or incentive pay. Total compensation will be well above base pay. If the person's work is classified as direct labor, would the additional increment be considered direct labor cost?

Strangely enough, many companies consider such additional employment costs as overhead. They do so partly for convenience, since it is often difficult to convert lump sum payments, per man or for the company as a whole, to the costs for each hour that an employee actually worked. Companies also consider these costs to be overhead because some costs, such as overtime, might unfairly penalize those products that happened to be in production when the cost was incurred.

Attaching Direct Labor Costs to Products

There are a number of ways that direct labor costs can be attached to products. One common method is for each worker to write down the time spent working on a product. Workers can do this in one of two ways.

1. A job ticket may accompany each job, which may be one item or a lot of 100 or 1,000 items. This ticket has a line for each operation. Workers write on this line the time they spent and perhaps also their names or employee numbers. When work on the product is completed, the job ticket records the times spent on each operation. A clerk (or computer) in the accounting office multiplies hours times the applicable rate to get the total direct labor cost.

   Some systems use multiple copies of the job ticket (one for each operation) or tickets with parts that can be torn off as each operation is completed. At the end of each day, the tickets or stubs representing work completed are sent to the accounting office for recording. Schedulers can use such an arrangement to record the jobs' progress. In more automated systems the job ticket might be a punched card that the worker inserts in a remote card reading machine located on the production floor. The machine reads the number of the job from the card, and the worker uses a keyboard on the machine to enter the operation number, the employee number, and the hours spent on the operation. This information then automatically goes into computer memory, so that a scheduler or salesperson can recall at any time the status of work-in-process. The card then moves on with the job to its next operation.

2. A slightly different system can be used to obtain job costs in situations where it is not feasible to attach a job ticket to a job, or where several employees work on the same job. In such situations workers enter on their time cards the jobs worked on during the day and the times spent on each. To collect labor hours by job, an accounting clerk sorts the time cards by job number.

Relating Indirect Labor to Products

Where labor costs are not direct, such as costs of machine adjusters or material handlers, a different system must be used. One method is to add up all indirect labor costs for a month or a year and to determine the ratio of indirect to direct labor costs for the same period. If in Department A indirect labor costs were $20,000 last year and direct labor $40,000, indirect labor could then be computed for each product at 50% of the actual direct labor cost.

Some manufacturing labor costs are not even direct to production departments. Costs of engineering, maintenance, scheduling, warehousing, and plant security are examples. Since these costs are also applied to products, they too are allocated, first to the production departments and then, along with other departmental indirect labor costs, to the products. We will discuss further the various ways of allocating indirect labor costs to products in the section of this chapter that describes allocation of overhead.

DEFINING THE COSTING UNIT

Defining the unit to which costs are to be applied can sometimes be a very troublesome area of cost accounting. Where a physical product is being produced, the costing unit is usually fairly clear. For example, a ton of steel, an electric motor, and a loaf of bread present few problems. However, an increasing proportion of our business activity produces services: transportation, communication, entertainment, recreation, medicine, law, finance, education. Cost accounting in these activities is difficult because the unit of output is often hard to define. To a railroad, a ton-mile for coal is not the same as a ton-mile for television sets. One minute of telephone conversation in New York City is different from a minute's talk in Charleston, West Virginia. Half-hour TV shows, surgical operations, and legal cases are not homogeneous items. Such service units don't make very good costing units. They need further definition or breakdown into smaller segments.

What is often required in service businesses is a more flexible approach to cost accounting. Since the main unit of output cannot generally be stocked in inventory, the cost accounting system is released from having to serve balance sheet requirements. Costing units can take any form that is useful to management, and since all costs are expensed each period, changes in the system will not be restrained by the need for consistency in inventory valuation.

Service activities within enterprises, such as purchasing, computing, and maintenance, as well as business that are entirely service, bring complex costing and control problems. More will be said about these in Part Four in the discussion of management control systems.

IDENTIFYING DIRECT MATERIAL COSTS

Material costs include both raw materials and purchased parts. After the initial introduction of material when work starts on a product, other material may be added at later stages. In an automobile manufacturing company, for example, a large number of purchased parts are added in the final stages of assembly.

It is usually easier with material than with labor to decide whether it should be considered a direct cost. If the material ends up in the final product, it will usually be considered direct. If it is applied only to one product but is destroyed in process, it would also generally be considered direct. But if the material is a small part of total cost, is used on a number of products, and is difficult to trace, it may be considered indirect and part of overhead. Indirect material is usually called *supplies* and includes such items as lubricants, cleaning materials, grinding wheels and glue.

Relating Material Costs To Products

Materials are often bought or requisitioned from storage directly for a specific product. The purchase order, requisition slip, or job ticket will record the information relating the material to a job or product. In this way the amount of material going into each product (batch, job, lot) is measured or counted.

Sometimes materials are put into production without being related to a product. Steel rods or sheet metal may be put on the production floor and used as needed. Or perhaps compounds are mixed from a variety of raw materials and sent through production, ending up in dozens of different end products. No one can say which end item a particular bit of raw material went into. In these instances, the cost of the material in the end product must be based on the quantity of each material required by design specifications to be in the product multiplied by the material's cost. That amount will then be added to the finished goods or cost of goods sold accounts. Determining whether the amount is accurate or not must await a check of inventories (work-in-process and raw materials) at the end of the period.

MANUFACTURING OVERHEAD

Manufacturing overhead,[1] which includes indirect labor and materials, is generally treated as a product cost, except in certain direct costing or variable costing systems that will be discussed in a later chapter. Overhead is added to the cost of direct labor and material to arrive at the total manufactured cost figure, which is used when costing inventory and calculating costs of goods sold. As products move through the production process, are worked on, and perhaps have material and components added, their cost increases. Some systems add labor, material, and overhead costs after each step; some wait until the item is finished before recognizing that it has acquired its full manufacturing cost. In any case the indirect nature of manufacturing overhead creates a special problem in discovering whatever connections there may be between the overhead cost and the benefit received by the end product.

---

[1] The term *overhead* usually means manufacturing overhead as distinguished from general administrative (overhead) expense and selling expense. Manufacturing overhead is also referred to as *burden*, and the term *indirect costs* usually refers to the same costs as are included in manufacturing overhead.

Since manufacturing overhead is allocated to products while general administrative overhead is not, an accounting system must clearly distinguish between the two. Most costs will clearly lie in one or the other category or *cost pool*, as it is often called, but some costs will fall into a gray area for which arguments can be made that costs should go either way.

Clearly, costs relating to running the production operation are part of manufacturing overhead. These costs would include

— production supervision: foremen, superintendents.
— indirect labor.
— supplies.
— factory heat, light, power, insurance, rent.
— quality control and manufacturing engineering.
— depreciation on the plant and equipment.
— maintenance and janitorial services.

Clearly, costs related to running the company but only indirectly related to running the plant are part of general administrative overhead. Some examples of these are

— president's salary.
— salaries of other officers and office staff, supplies, and cost of occupancy.
— financial, legal, and corporate accounting costs.
— research and engineering costs not directly related to production.

In the gray area are certain product development costs, costs of accounting and record-keeping, and costs that may be shared by headquarters and plant, such as the costs of building maintenance, utilities, security, and the computer. Some logical method must be developed to allocate these costs to either general administration or manufacturing overhead. And once the system is established, it must be followed consistently, both in planning or budgeting costs and in computing actual costs for the period.

Allocating Manufacturing Overhead to Products

Since manufacturing overhead is not a direct expense and not directly traceable to a product, accountants usually distribute it to products on top of a direct expense as a predetermined percentage of that expense. Labor is the most frequently used direct expense base, although occasionally material costs, a combination of expenses, or a direct measure of activity, such as machine hours, may also be used.

The procedure is to project a relationship between the overhead and the direct expense used as a base and to use that relationship for each product. For example, consider a small manufacturing plant. Total direct labor for next year is expected to be $120,000 and manufacturing overhead to be $180,000. For every dollar of direct labor expended on a job, $1.50 is tacked on to cover overhead. If Product A requires $7.00 of direct labor, $10.50 of overhead will be added. Product A's material cost of $5.00 will be added to the $7.00 labor cost and the $10.50 overhead to arrive at a total manufacturing cost of $22.50. This amount is added to inventory and the $10.50 is called *absorbed overhead*. It is the amount of overhead incorporated into inventory.

To set up the relationship of $1.50 in overhead for each dollar of direct labor, we had to estimate the amount expected to be spent on both direct labor and manufacturing overhead. This estimate is usually made a year at a time, so that the $1.50 or 150% overhead rate would be in effect for a year before being revised. This process usually starts with a sales estimate, which is then converted to required production volume. The required overhead and direct costs are then projected to meet that volume.

One can readily see that for any specific accounting period, the amount of overhead absorbed into inventory using the overhead rate may be different from the actual amount of overhead incurred. This discrepancy would arise if either total actual direct labor or total actual overhead (or both) were not as estimated. For example, in the following situation the overhead rate was $1.50 per direct labor dollar:

	Direct Labor	Absorbed Overhead	Actual Overhead	Over or (Under) Absorbed Overhead
Estimate for 1981..............	120,000	180,000	180,000	0
Estimate for each month........	10,000	15,000	15,000	0
Actual for January 1981........	10,000	15,000	16,000	(1,000)
Actual for February 1981.......	10,000	15,000	14,500	500
Actual for March 1981.........	8,000	12,000	14,000	(2,000)
Actual for April 1981..........	12,000	18,000	16,500	1,500

The right hand column tells management whether more (or less) overhead was absorbed into inventory than was actually spent. This information tells management whether the estimated relationship ($1.50 per direct labor dollar) was born out by actual results; but if it was not, further analysis will be needed to find out why. This kind of review is called *variance analysis* and will be discussed in Chapter 5 on standard costing.

Allocation of Overhead to Departments

The previous discussion examined the process of allocating overhead to products. In practice it is usually not as simple as that discussion implied. In a company of any size the allocation will be done in stages. General manufacturing overhead, such as plant administration and utilities, will be distributed to departments, some of which are production departments, but some are service departments such as maintenance or manufacturing engineering. The total cost of running these service departments, some being direct and some coming from general manufacturing overhead, will then be further distributed to production departments. The final step will be an allocation to products, using an overhead rate based on a direct cost such as direct labor.

Allocating overhead to a department or distributing a service department's cost to a production department can be done using several different kinds of bases:

Overhead Cost Pool	_Base Used_
Plant Administration	Number of people in the department's payroll.
Heat	Square footage of space used by each department.
Equipment Maintenance	Capital cost of machinery in place in each department.
Electric Power	Combination of square footage and machine horsepower in each department.
Computer Cost	Actual usage by departments.

The rationale used in choosing a base for allocating overhead usually considers the following criteria:

1. Benefit. The department that receives the most benefit is charged the most. Maintenance is a good example of such a benefit.

2. Variability of usage. If overhead varies with a measure of activity, that measure of activity is used as a base. Supplemental employee benefits usually vary with payroll.

3. Traceability. If an item of overhead can be traced to a department, even though benefit and variability may be indistinguishable, that department is charged.

4. Fairness. For some overhead items there is no clear benefit, variability, or traceability. In these instances whatever method seems fair is generally used.

5. Simplicity. An overly complex procedure is both expensive and confusing. Sometimes the simplest way is best.

The basic purpose of allocating overhead is to arrive at a total manufacturing cost. That total cost figure may be used in many ways, such as to provide a basis for pricing, to estimate costs of expended production, or to modify a product line. It is also the basis for valuation of inventory and cost of goods sold. Because there are many acceptable ways of allocating overhead, and because overhead itself is an indirect expense and hence will not vary directly with volume or product changes, the resulting total cost figure should be used with caution in predicting overall cost changes. The next chapter on relevant costs will examine more fully the use of costs in various management decisions.

JOB COSTING AND PROCESS COSTING

Having reviewed the general procedure for relating costs to products, let us now examine more specifically the two primary ways this can be carried out: job costing and process costing. Job costing systems are most useful where there are distinct units or production, such as customer's order, a production lot of 1,000 pieces for inventory, or one office building. Work on each of these jobs has a clear beginning and ending, and frequently the job requires a unique set of operations that differentiate it from other jobs.

Process costing systems are used where production is continuous and there are no jobs requiring a different set of operations. Thus, oil refineries, flour mills, electrical generating plants, and chemical processing businesses are likely to use process costing systems.

Job Costing Systems

In job costing, records are kept showing how much material and labor went toward making each job, batch, or order. Overhead may then be added on as a percent of labor or of some other direct cost base. When the job is finished, management can know fairly accurately what an item actually costs. Of course, if overhead is over- or under-absorbed during the period, the overhead applied to each job will not be correct. However, aside from that limitation, job cost systems that record actual material and labor quantities produce fairly accurate costs per job.

The core of a job costing system is the *job sheet*. On this form are recorded the actual amounts of material, labor and overhead expended on a job. A simplified job sheet is illustrated below.

```
                                    Job Sheet
                                    ─────────
    Job No.  ___437___
    Date started      __4/5/77__
    Date finished     __4/8/77__

    Materials:
    Bar stock         ___250___   feet at  $__4.00__  Extension  $_1,000.00_
    Sheet stock       ___35____   feet at  $__9.00__              __315.00__
    Fittings          __2,024__   no. at   $___.85__             _1,721.00_

    Labor:
    Dept. A           ___17____   hrs. at  $__6.30__              __107.00__
    Dept. B           ____5____   hrs. at  $__4.35__              ___21.75__

    Overhead:
    Dept. A      212% of labor dollars                           __227.05__
    Dept. B      145% of labor dollars                           ___31.54__

    Total Manufacturing Cost                               $ 3,423.44

    Number of good pieces completed ___1,000___   Cost per piece  $___3.42___
```

There are many varieties of job costing systems. The system used in the construction industry for highways, buildings, or ships accumulates vast numbers of different costs over long periods of time, often more than a year. When the project is finished, a review can be made to see how costs came out in relation to the costs estimated at the time of the original bid. Though an identical project would probably not be encountered again, parts of projects (laying brick, welding plates, or excavating dirt) are often sufficiently similar from one job to the next to make past cost records helpful in predicting costs of future operations.

Other job costing systems are much smaller in scope. A machine shop may have many jobs in process at one time, and each worker and machine may be devoted to several jobs in the course of a day. The objective is still the same: to record actual times and costs spent on each job.

In some situations it is helpful to have a standard rate per machine-hour which includes both labor and overhead costs. Actual hours spent on each job are recorded and multiplied by this rate. Printing companies often use this type of system, using a preset hourly rate for linotype, presswork, or binding. Like overhead, the actual costs of running the linotype and presses may be over or under the costs absorbed by the jobs. However, the printer wants to be able to send his bill out quickly and does not want to wait until the month-end closing tells him what the actual costs were. Hence, the standard rate for each operation applied to actual hours spent on the job is often the best way of quickly determining a fairly accurate cost.

Process Costing Systems

In a process costing system the cost of running a production facility for a given length of time is divided by the number of units produced in the period to obtain a production cost per unit. The length of time is usually fairly long, perhaps a week or a month, but it can be any length. This type of system is most useful in situations where similar items are produced for long periods of time.

In job costing systems, production costs are collected for work done on a job, which may be one piece of work or a batch of 1,000 similar items. The job defines the limits of cost applicability. Material and direct labor used on the job or batch are measured and costed. Overhead is usually applied as a percentage of direct labor.

In process costing the "job" is the production work accomplished during a period of time. The time period, therefore, defines the costing unit.

Process costing systems tend to be used or large production facilities designed to produce one product. In such instances all costs associated with the facility are direct to the product. Most of manufacturing overhead, for example, will be direct cost. If a flour mill produces one type of flour, all costs of the mill—direct labor, depreciation, supplies, and the superintendent—are direct costs. One should note, however, that though they are direct, they are not necessarily variable with volume.

Process costing can also be used for small operations. A single punch press may work continuously on one component used in a variety of end products made by a company. The cost of running the press for a month divided by the pieces produced would be the cost per piece.

Job costing systems can also be found in both small and large operations. Job costing can be used with small jobs, as would be found in a machine shop or printing company. In such business, a man or machine will complete one job and start another within a day or at least every few days. However, job costing can also be used with large jobs, such as construction projects or shipbuilding. A job in these businesses may well last over a year.

A company is sometimes faced with a decision whether to shift from a process to a job cost system. For example, if a paper company decides to expand its line from one grade of paper to several, and because of differing machine speeds, wants to know the costs for each grade, it will probably collect the times spent on each grade. What had been a system that computed the unit cost of a month's production becomes a system of computing the unit cost per grade. The *job* becomes that which was produced in the time spent on each grade.

A decision to go the other way, from job costing to process costing, may also be made on occasion. A department that produces a variety of small stamped parts that are costed by batches may find that costing is simpler if total department costs are related to pounds of stampings produced per month. If the stampings are sufficiently similar, the result will be almost as accurate as job costing, and it will no longer be necessary to record the time spent on each part.

Partially Completed Production

In a machine shop using a job costing system, there are likely to be partly completed jobs at the beginning and end of each month. In such a situation overhead is normally absorbed by this work-in-process according to the amount of work done on each job. A job with ten labor hours expended on it would absorb $15 of overhead if $1.50 per labor hour were the applicable overhead rate. If 20 labor hours are used the following month to finish the job, it will absorb another $30 of overhead the next month and be put into finished goods inventory with a total of $45 of overhead included in its cost.

Thus, in job costing systems there is no particular problem in accounting for partially completed jobs. With process costing systems this accounting is more difficult, and it may be necessary to use *equivalent units of production* to determine how much cost should be absorbed by partially completed production.

Equivalent Units of Production

In process costing the actual cost of units produced is computed by relating cost inputs for the period to unit outputs for the period. If work in process changes significantly, the cost per unit computed in this way can be distorted. If an increase in work-in-process is not recognized, the cost per unit of output will be too high, because much of the cost incurred during the period went toward that increase in work-in-process, and only some of the cost incurred went into the units completed.

In process costing systems, when inventory changes are expected to be significant, equivalent units of production are often used to compensate. This method considers the amount of work-in-process and its extent of completion at the beginning and at the end of the period. If 4,000 units were three quarters finished at the beginning, they represented 3,000 equivalent units. If at the end there are 8,000 units, half finished, they represent 4,000 equivalent units. The work actually done during the period was

1.   To finish the partly completed beginning inventory of 4,000 units.

2.   To start and finish 3,000 units.

3.   To do some work on 8,000 more units so that they are half finished.

The diagram below shows this work graphically.

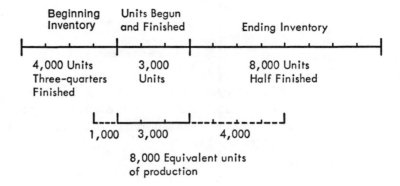

The accounting process would compute the equivalent units as follows:

Units transferred to finished goods.................		7,000
Minus equivalent units in beginning inventory.........	—	3,000
Plus equivalent units in ending inventory.............	+	4,000
Gives equivalent units of production for the period....		8,000.

Material cost will also be part of this computation. In many instances material cost and labor cost are added at different times. Material may all be added at the start, while labor may be added during the process. Thus, the material equivalent units of production may well differ from the labor equivalent units in the same period. Consequently, labor and material are usually handled in separate computations.

SUMMARY   We have reviewed three ways of classifying and organizing costs:

1.   By function (labor, material, overhead).

2.   By organizational unit (costs of a plating department).

3.   By product or service.

Whereas the functional classification is a useful starting point, the other two classifications provide the type of cost information most directly related to managerial decisions.

Developing costs by organizational unit is useful for cost control, for such costs can be assigned to areas of responsibility. Product costs, on the other hand, are necessary for pricing decisions and profitability evaluations.

The following diagram summarizes the flow of costs in manufacturing and services activities.

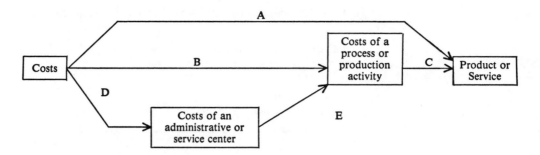

A. Some costs can be traced directly to a product or service. Material and direct labor are common examples. These costs are direct because one can measure the amount of material or hours of labor used for each unit of product or service.

B. Some costs can be traced directly to a process or production activity, but not to a specific product or service. Ink or depreciation for a printing press, drivers for a delivery route are examples.

C. The cost of the process or production activity can then be distributed to products or services. Often this is done using direct labor hours as a base. A rate per direct labor hour is established and the number of labor hours used by the product or service determines the amount of indirect costs assigned to that product or service.

    With a job costing system, some costs are direct (distributed via route A) and some indirect and use route B and C. A process costing system, on the other hand, does not use route A. The process costs are accumulated for a period of time and distributed to units of product by dividing the total process costs by the units produced during the period. Thus, in a job costing system a unit cost is made up of some direct costs plus an average indirect cost; in a process costing system, the cost of a unit of product is entirely an average for the period of time.

D. Some indirect costs may go through an additional distribution step. Certain administrative and service costs, such as occupancy or maintenance costs, may not be traceable directly to a process or production center. They are assigned first to the activity center via route D.

E. Costs for the administrative or service activity are accumulated and then assigned to production or process centers using an allocation base. Occupancy costs would probably use square feet, personnel and administrative costs might use the number of people, and maintenance costs might use the value of the equipment. In some cases the assignment can be a direct charge, such as repair hours used by each department times a cost per hour.

    In a job costing system a high proportion of costs follow the direct A route, with some costs following the BC and DEC routes. With process costing, all costs follow the BC and DEC routes.

Relevant Cost Analysis: Economic Analysis for Business Decisions

Skillful decision making is an art. But this art is based on knowledge of revenue and cost behavior. Costs are meaningful only in the light of specific assumptions and conditions. Thus, many different concepts of cost exist and yield varying cost figures. Understanding these concepts and using them appropriately in problem situations is termed *relevant cost analysis*. Actually, relevant cost analysis covers revenues as well as costs. Hence this chapter has the more general subtitle "Economic Analysis for Business Decisions."

COST BEHAVIOR: FIXED AND VARIABLE COSTS

The cost of a manufactured product or service is composed of many different elements. These cost elements behave differently under varying circumstances. One of the most important circumstances affecting cost behavior is the volume or quantity of goods or services produced. Some costs vary directly with volume and are called *variable costs*. For example, the cost of steel in automobiles, food in a restaurant, or coal for a power company are variable costs in that the quantity of steel, food, or coal used is directly related to the quantity of automobiles produced, meals served, or kilowatts generated. It should be noted that the total amount of variable cost changes with volume, but the cost per unit remains the same. The cost of the steel in each car will be the same whether 50,000 or 60,000 are produced. Other costs do not vary directly with the quantity produced and are called *fixed costs*. The plant manager's salary in the auto factory, the cost of the restaurant's rent, and the depreciation of the electrical generator are examples of costs that do not change as the level of output changes. Some cost elements are neither fixed nor variable—these will be discussed later in this chapter.

The decision maker must study each situation fully to determine the nature and significance of each cost element. The impact of volume on cost behavior can be seen in the following example from the Sunshine Manufacturing Company. Study this example carefully, for it will be used throughout this chapter to illustrate a number of relevant cost concepts.

Sunshine makes two types of Zingos—Model A, costing $32.50 and Model B, costing $57.00. Figure 3-1 shows the company's analysis that determined these costs.

Figure 3-1

SUNSHINE MANUFACTURING CO.
Cost Report
(Full Cost Basis)

		A Zingos		B Zingos
Production Volume		20,000		5,000
Cost Elements				
Raw materials and purchased parts		$ 8.00		$11.00
Direct Labor:				
Fabrication	1.50		2.00	
Assembly	1.50		4.00	
Testing, packaging	1.00	4.00	2.00	8.00
Manufacturing Overhead:				
Indirect Labor	2.00		4.00	
Supplies	3.00		4.00	
Depreciation—building	6.00		12.00	
Depreciation—equipment	1.50		2.00	
Utilities and all other items	8.00	20.50	16.00	38.00
Total Cost		$32.50		$57.00

The costs shown in Figure 3-1 are called *full costs* because they include all manufacturing costs.[1] This cost analysis covers the following elements:

1. *Raw Materials and Purchased Parts*. These are the estimated costs of the steel, plastic, wiring, and purchased parts included in each Zingo. They are clearly variable, because as the production level increases, more of these items must be purchased and used.

---

[1] The alternative method is called *direct costing* or *variable costing*, in which case only variable costs are allocated to the product. This costing method will be discussed in Chapter 6.

2. *Direct Labor.* These cost elements reflect the labor payrolls in each of the three departments: fabrication, assembly and final test, and packing. These costs are also variable, because more men must be added to the departments as the production level is increased. If production levels are reduced, the workforce is cut back.

3. *Indirect Labor.* These costs include money spent for supervisors, material handlers, utility relief people, and clean-up crews. As explained in Chapter 2 these are indirect costs because they cannot be tied definitely to a particular product or job. Nevertheless, Sunshine considers these indirect labor costs to be variable with volume, because as production increases and more direct laborers are hired, Sunshine must also hire more supervisors, material handlers, and so on. From past experience Sunshine determined that its indirect payroll is about half its direct payroll. Since management expected this relationship to hold over normal operating levels, they allocated $1.00 of indirect labor for every $2.00 of direct labor used to make Zingos.

4. *Supplies.* Supplies are also variable. They include the cost of paint, packaging material, and miscellaneous items that, while difficult to measure by items produced, do vary with level of production.

   The cost of supplies shown in Figure 3-1 was determined by plotting the past cost of supplies against production volume month-by-month on a graph. Volume was measured not in absolute units but in labor dollars, because that measure reflected more adequately the larger size and production time of Model B Zingos. This graphical analysis revealed that for every $1.00 of direct labor, Sunshine spent about 75¢ on supplies for Model A Zingos and 50¢ for Model B Zingos. Thus, Model A Zingos, with $4.00 direct labor, were allocated $3.00 of supplies per Zingo while Model B's, with $8.00 direct labor, were allocated $4.00 of supplies.

5. *Depreciation of the Building.* The factory building had originally cost $3.6 million to construct and had an expected useful life of 20 years. Accordingly, $180,000 depreciation expense was charged to manufacturing each year. Depreciation was also allocated to products on the basis of volume, again measured in terms of labor content. However, depreciation was a fixed cost. The depreciation cost per Zingo depended upon the number of Zingos produced. Accordingly, each year an estimate was made of production volume and this estimate (called planned or normal volume) was used to determine the depreciation cost of Zingos. These calculations were as follows:

Zingo Model	Normal Volume (units)	Direct Labor Content (per units)	Volume Expressed in Labor Dollars
A	20,000	$4.00	$ 80,000
B	5,000	8.00	40,000
			$120,000

Therefore,

$$\frac{\text{Yearly Depreciation Cost}}{\text{Expected Yearly Volume}} = \frac{\$180,000}{\$120,000} = 150\%$$

or a depreciation rate of 150% of direct labor. Thus, the cost of building depreciation for Model A was set at $6.00 (150% × $4.00) and for Model B at $12.00 per Zingo.

6. *Depreciation of Equipment.* The depreciation cost for the equipment, though also a fixed cost, was allocated to products differently. Since all of the equipment was in the fabrication department, Sunshine decided to allocate the depreciation cost of this equipment to products on the basis of volume *in the fabrication department alone*—volume was again measured in labor dollars.
   Sunshine's calculations were as follows:

Zingo Model	Normal Volume	Fabrication Direct Labor Content	Volume Expressed in Fabrication Labor Dollars
A	20,000	$1.50	$30,000
B	5,000	2.00	10,000
			$40,000

Since the yearly depreciation cost was $40,000, the depreciation rate was 100% as applied to fabrication labor:

$$\frac{\text{Yearly Depreciation Cost}}{\text{Expected Yearly Volume}} = \frac{\$40,000}{\$40,000} = 100\%.$$

Thus, the equipment depreciation cost for Model A was $1.50 (100% × $1.50) and for Model B was $2.00.

7. *Utilities and all other items.* This entry included the costs of heat, light, power, telephone, taxes, that plant manager's office costs and salary, and other miscellaneous items. These costs were essentially fixed, because experience had shown that they were insensitive to changes in production level. Sunshine incurred costs of $240,000 per year in this category, and management was convinced that these costs would be substantially the same whether 25,000 Zingos were produced or 10,000 or 50,000.
   These utilities and other costs were allocated to products in the same manner as was building depreciation. Since these costs were expected to be $240,000 per year, the overhead rate for these utility accounts was 200% of total direct labor content.

Thus, by stating all cost elements as a cost per Zingo, Sunshine was able to construct the full cost of each model Zingo as shown in Figure 3-1. This cost remained a good estimate as long as volume was close to the expected level. But if volume were different, a new kind of cost analysis was needed. To make this analysis the cost elements were restated as in Figure 3-2.

Figure 3-2

SUNSHINE MANUFACTURING COMPANY
Cost Report
(Showing Fixed and Variable Elements)

	Variable costs		
	A Zingos	B Zingos	Fixed cost
Raw Materials and Purchase Parts	$ 8.00	$11.00	$ 0
Direct Labor:			
Fabrication	1.50	2.00	0
Assembly	1.50	4.00	0
Testing, packaging	1.00	2.00	0
Manufacturing Overhead:			
Indirect Labor	2.00	4.00	0
Supplies	3.00	4.00	0
Depreciation—building	0	0	180,000
Depreciation—equipment	0	0	40,000
Utilities and all other items	0	0	240,000
Total Costs	$17.00	$27.00	$460,000

Thus, the variable costs for A and B Zingos are $17.00 and $27.00, respectively, and fixed costs are $460,000. It should be clear to the reader that Figures 3-1 and 3-2 portray the same basic facts. With the assumed volume of 25,000 Zingos,

Model	Projected Volume
A	20,000
B	5,000
Total	25,000

the projected manufacturing costs would be $935,000 according to the full cost data shown in Figure 3-1.

Model	Full Cost	×	Volume	=	Total Costs
A	$32.50		20,000		$650,000
B	57.00		5,000		285,000
					$935,000

Happily, the same $935,000 projected cost figure could be obtained from the fixed and variable cost elements in Figure 3-2.

Model	Variable Cost	×	Volume	=	Total Variable Cost
A	$17.50		20,000		$340,000
B	27.00		5,000		135,000
					475,000
				Plus Fixed Costs	460,000
				Total Costs	$935,000

PROFIT PLANNING WITH FIXED AND VARIABLE COSTS

Currently, A and B Zingos sell for $50.00 and $65.00, respectively. The market research group estimates that sales volume will increase to 35,000 units if prices are lowered. The situation is as follows:

Model	Price	Projected Volume (units)
A	$50	20,000
B	65	5,000
		25,000

Market research recommends these prices and volumes:

Model	Suggested Price	Projected Volume (units)
A	$45	25,000
B	60	10,000
		35,000

If prices are lowered but volume is increased, as suggested, will profits increase? This is the decision to be made. It can be approached in a variety of ways. There is also a *wrong* way to attempt to solve this problem.

The first thing to do is to determine the profits under the current pricing system. They are shown in Figure 3-3 computed in three different ways.

Figure 3-3 Projected Profits With Existing Prices

1. **Full cost method**

Model	Sales price	−	Full cost	=	Profit margin	×	Estimated volume	=	Projected profits
A	$50		$32.50		$17.50		20,000		$350,000
B	65		57.00		8.00		5,000		40,000
									$390,000

2. **Variable cost method**

Model	Price	−	Variable cost	=	Gross profit margin	×	Estimated volume	=	Gross profits
A	$50		$17		33		20,000		$660,000
B	65		27		38		5,000		190,000
									$850,000
							Less Fixed Cost		− 460,000
							Total Profit		$390,000

3. **Total sales less total cost method**

Model	Sales price	×	Volume	=	Total sales
A	$50		20,000		$1,000,000
B	65		5,000		325,000
					$1,325,000
			Less: Total Costs		− 935,000
			Total Profits		$ 390,000

Under the *full cost method*, the full cost per unit is subtracted from the sales price to get the profit per unit, which is then multiplied by the projected volume of units to get the total profit. Under the *variable cost method*, the variable costs per unit are subtracted from the selling price to get the gross margin per unit. This gross margin is then multiplied by the project volume to get total gross profit. From the sum of the gross profits for each model the total fixed costs are subtracted to yield total profit. Under the *total sales less total cost method*, the total sales are first determined by multiplying the sales price by the projected volume. Next, the total costs (determined by either of the two methods discussed previously) are subtracted to yield total profit.

Before calculating the expected profits under the revised price and volume conditions, we will first look at a wrong way of attacking this problem and see why it's wrong. Figure 3-4 shows a projected profit of $342,500 at the new price and volume levels. Since this amount is less than the $390,000 profits under the existing conditions, we would be tempted to reject the market research group's recommendation. But Figure 3-4 is wrong. The full cost data in Figure 3-1 *cannot* be used to project the total cost at this new level of production, because those cost figures were based upon the old, lower estimates of volume. Costs must be recalculated as shown in Figure 3-5 because both per-unit costs and total costs will change as volume is increased.

**Figure 3-4
Projected Profits
With Revised
Prices—the Wrong
Way**

Model	Sales price	−	Cost	=	Profit margin	×	Estimated volume	=	Profit
A	$45		$32.50		$12.50		25,000		$312,500
B	60		57.00		3.00		10,000		30,000
									$342,500

Because of the increased volume, the overhead rate for building depreciation drops from 150% to 100%. The overhead rates for equipment depreciation and for utilities, the other fixed costs, also drop. As a result, the new full costs for A and B become $27.37 and $47.06. This change illustrates two very important aspects of full costs. First, whenever there are fixed cost elements, certain assumptions must be made about expected volume and the method of cost allocation be determined, before full cost figures can be established. Second, whenever volume changes, so do the full costs per unit.

The reader will note that the revisions shown in Figure 3-5 required a lengthy set of calculations and considerable time to complete. Another set of volume projections would require a similar effort. If there were many products and many possible levels of volume under consideration, nothing short of a computer could perform all of the calculations necessary to budget total profit.

Fortunately, there is an easier way. The fixed and variable cost elements from Figure 3-2 can be used to make the total cost calculations very quickly.

Figure 3-5

SUNSHINE MANUFACTURING COMPANY
Cost Report with Revised Production Volume
(Full Cost Basis)

	A Zingos	B Zingos	Explanation of revisions
Production Volume	25,000	10,000	
Cost Elements			
Raw Materials, etc.	$ 8.00	$11.00	No Change
Direct Labor (Total Manufacturing Overhead):	4.00	8.00	No Change
Indirect Labor	2.00	4.00	No Change
Supplies	3.00	4.00	No Change
Depreciation—building	4.00	8.00	See Note A
Depreciation—equipment	1.04	1.39	See Note B
Utilities and all other items	5.33	10.67	See Note C
TOTAL COSTS	$27.37	$47.06	

Note A: Revised Calculation of Building Depreciation Rate

Model	Revised volume	Direct labor content	Volume expressed in labor dollars
A	25,000 units	$4.00	$100,000
B	10,000 units	8.00	80,000
			$180,000

$$\frac{\text{Yearly depreciation cost}}{\text{Revised yearly volume}} = \frac{\$180,000}{\$180,000} = 100\%$$

Therefore building depreciation cost for Model A is 100% of $4.00 direct labor cost, and for Model B is 100% of $8.00 direct labor cost.

Note B: Revised Calculation of Equipment Depreciation Rate

Model	Revised volume	Fabrication direct labor	Volume expressed in fabrication labor dollars
A	25,000 units	$1.50	$37,500
B	10,000 units	2.00	20,000
			$57,500

$$\frac{\text{Yearly depreciation cost}}{\text{Revised fabrication volume}} = \frac{\$40,000}{\$57,500} = 69.5\%$$

Model A: 69.5% of $1.50 = $1.04;
Model B: 69.5% of $2.00 = $1.39

Note C: Revised Calculation of Utilities, etc. Rate

$$\frac{\text{Yearly depreciation cost}}{\text{Revised yearly volume}} = \frac{\$240,000}{\$180,000} = 133.3\%$$

Model A: 133.3% of $4.00 = $5.33;
Model B: 133.3% of $8.00 = $10.67

With these new per unit cost figures, the total cost at the new volume can be calculated:

Model	Full cost	×	Volume	=	Total cost
A	$27.37		25,000		$ 684,250
B	47.06		10,000		470,000
					$1,154,850

Model	Variable cost ×	New volume =	Total Variable Cost
A	$17.00	25,000	$ 425,000
B	27.00	10,000	270,000
			$ 695,000
		Plus: Fixed costs	460,000
		Total cost	$1,155,000*

* The slight difference between the $1,155,000 and the $1,154,850 is
from rounding.

With these new figures, the project profits at the new sales price and
volumes can easily be determined by any of the methods previously discussed. These calculations are shown in Figure 3-6 and show identical results.[2]

These profits are much higher. Thus, in the absence of any other data,
Sunshine should accept the market research group's recommendations and
reduce its prices.

**Figure 3-6
Projected Profits
With Revised
Prices and
Volumes**

Full Cost Method

Model	Price —	Revised Full cost =	Profit margin ×	Estimated volume =	Projected profits
A	$45	$27.37	$17.63	25,000	$440,750
B	60	47.06	12.94	10,000	129,400
					$570,150

Variable Cost Method

Model	Price —	Variable cost =	Gross profit margin ×	Estimated volume =	Gross profit
A	$45	$17	$28	25,000	$ 700,000
B	60	27	33	10,000	330,000
					$1,030,000
				Less: Fixed Cost	460,000
				Total Profit	$ 570,000

Total Sales—Total Cost Method

Model	Sales price ×	Volume =	Total sales
A	$45	25,000	$1,125,000
B	60	10,000	600,000
			$1,725,000
		Less: Total Costs	1,155,000
		Total Profit	$ 570,000

CONTRIBUTION

The terms *contribution* or *marginal contribution* or *contribution to
overhead and profit* have essentially the same meaning. Contribution is the
difference between the selling price of a product or service and its variable
costs; it is the amount of funds available to cover the fixed costs and to provide a profit. If the selling prices of A and B Zingos are $50.00 and $65.00,
respectively, contribution is calculated as follows:

[2] Again, the slight differences in results are due to the fact that the revised full cost figures are rounded
numbers.

	A	B
Sales Price	$50.00	$65.00
Less Variable Costs:		
Materials	8.00	11.00
Direct Labor	4.00	8.00
Total Variable Cost	5.00	8.00
	17.00	27.00
Contribution	$33.00	$38.00

Contribution is not the same as profit, if there are fixed costs. The relationship between contribution and profit can be illustrated in several ways. One method is the per-unit calculation, as shown in Figure 3-7.

Figure 3-7

	A	B
Sales Price	$50.00	$65.00
Less Variable Cost	17.00	27.00
Contribution	33.00	38.00
Less Fixed Costs*	15.50	30.00
Profit/Unit	$17.50	$ 8.00

* Assuming an estimated volume of 20,000 and 5,000 units as shown in Figure 3–1.

A second method shows the relationship in terms of total dollars, as shown in Figure 3-8.

Figure 3-8

	A	B	Total
Sales Price	$ 50.00	$65.00	
Less Variable Cost	17.00	27.00	
Contribution/unit	$ 33.00	$38.00	
× Volume	20,000	5,000	
Total Contribution	$660,000	$190,000	$850,000
Less Fixed Cost			460,000
Total Profit			$390,000

Contribution has many uses in business decision making. The effect on profit of changes in selling price, in unit volume, or in variable cost can easily and quickly be seen by determining the change in contribution. For example, take the situation depicted in Figure 3-8. Suppose that the unit volume of B Zingos is 8,000 rather than 5,000. What's the effect on total profit? Clearly, we would be adding an extra 3,000 units at $38.00 contribution per unit or $114,000 to profit. Suppose instead that the selling price of Model B falls by $8.00. What happens to profit? Here the decrease in contribution is $8.00 per unit times 5,000 units or $40,000. We'll see other examples in this chapter of how the concept of contribution aids the decision maker.

DECISION MAKING: RELEVANT COSTS

The accounting rules for preparing financial statements such as the income statement and the balance sheet require that costs be handled in certain prescribed ways. In accordance with these rules, product and service costs are calculated as shown in Figure 3-1. Unfortunately, such cost determinations are rarely the "right" costs to use in a decision-making situation. One must get behind such calculations to determine what cost figures are really relevant for a particular decision. We can illustrate this process with the information we now possess concerning Sunshine Manufacturing.

Suppose that the selling price of Model B Zingos drops to $55.00, due to competition. Since Figure 3-1 shows the full manufactured cost of these products as $57.00, the question of dropping Model B is immediately raised. Why sell at a loss? If one works just with the data in Figure 3-1, one has no question—the product should be dropped. Otherwise, Sunshine will lose $10,000:

New Sales Price......................	$ 55.00
Cost.................................	57.00
Loss/Unit...........................	$ 2.00
× Projected Volume..................	5,000
Expected Loss......................	$10,000.

But there is more to this matter than first meets the eye.

One approach to this problem is to predict changes in revenue and costs. If the product is dropped—what items will be affected? A *differential analysis* can be set up as in Figure 3-9.

Figure 3-9 Differential Analysis

	Keep model B (5,000 units)	Drop model B	Differences
Revenue			
Sales........................	$275,000	$ 0	($275,000)
Costs			
Materials	$ 55,000	0	$ 55,000
Direct Labor	40,000	0	40,000
Indirect Labor	20,000	0	20,000
Supplies	20,000	0	20,000
Depreciation—building	60,000	60,000	0
Depreciation—equipment	10,000	10,000	0
Utilities and all other items........	80,000	80,000	0
Total Costs	$285,000	$150,000	$135,000
Net profit and difference	($ 10,000)	($150,000)	($140,000)

Thus, in summary, if Model B is dropped, the relevant items are

Lost Revenue..... ....$275,000
Cost Savings.........................135,000
Net Decrease in Profit................ $140,000.

Here we see that rather than lose $10,000 by keeping Model B, Sunshine would actually lose $150,000 by dropping Model B!

How does this discrepancy arise? The reader will note that certain cost elements have been eliminated from consideration in this differential analysis. Depreciation and utility costs have been excluded because they are fixed costs—costs that will remain and must be incurred by Sunshine whether Product B is produced or not. These costs will not be saved if the product is dropped. For purposes of this decision, these costs are "sunk"; they cannot be affected by the decision to keep or drop.

The decision to keep Model B or drop it is sometimes called a *keep or drop* problem. In addition to the differential analysis discussed previously, a total cost analysis of such problems may be made. Figure 3-9 shows that after total costs, there will be a $10,000 loss if Model B is kept, but that $150,000 of costs will still be incurred even if the product is dropped. In the absence of a new product to take the place of B, these $150,000 of costs would have to be charged to Product A. Such a reallocation of costs should not be allowed to confuse the central issue: whatever the profits are on the rest of Sunshine's business, they will be $10,000 lower if Model B is kept and $150,000 lower if Model B is dropped. Clearly, Sunshine will be better off by $140,000 by keeping Model B, even if Model B loses $10,000 at the new price.

Some managers study these keep or drop problems using a contribution basis as illustrated in Figure 3-10.

**Figure 3-10
Contribution
Analysis**

Sales Price		$ 55.00
Less out-of-pocket cost		
Material	$11.00	
Labor	8.00	
Out-of-pocket overhead	8.00	27.00
Contribution/unit		$ 28.00
× Volume		× 5,000 units
Total loss if product dropped		$140,000

**ACCOUNTING
FOR SUNK
COSTS**

You may still be thinking about those sunk costs that were ignored. Are they not real costs? If so, do they not show up somewhere? After all, buildings and equipment are being carried on the balance sheet as assets and must be expensed to the income statement sometime. Perhaps another example will clear things up.

Suppose that Red Ball Freight Line had just installed a $5,000 gasoline engine in one of their trucks when a new diesel engine costing $7,000 reached the market. Either engine would outlast the remaining useful life of the truck and would have a negligible salvage value. Expected fuel consumption over the remaining life of the truck would be about 50,000 gallons for the gasoline-powered engine, but only 42,500 gallons for the newer engine. Both fuels were expected to cost $1.30/gallon. Red Ball management was sorry that it had not heard of the new diesel before installing the gasoline engine, because the fuel savings would have more than offset the additional cost of the new engine.

Indeed, it was too bad that management had not heard of the new engine sooner—but perhaps there was still a saving to be made. Suppose that the extra cost of removing the gas engine and installing the new diesel was just equal to the resale value of the gas engine—$500. Should Sunshine have switched? The conventional bookkeeping answer would have been *no*, as is shown in Figure 3-11

Figure 3-11 Bookkeeper's Approach—Red Ball Problem

Cost of new diesel engine	$7,000
Loss on sale of gas engine ($5,000-$500)	4,500
Installation cost	500
Total Cost	$12,000
Savings on fuel 7,500 gallons × $1.30/gallon	9,750
Total Loss	(2,250)

But this answer is wrong! Again look at just what differences there would be if the new engine were acquired. Clearly, the investment in the gasoline engine is a sunk cost, as is shown by the out-of-pocket or cash flow analysis of Figure 3-12

Figure 3-12 Cash Flow Analysis—Red Ball Problem

Cash outflows	
Cost of new diesel engine	$ 7,000
Installation cost	500
Total Cash Outflow	$ 7,500
Cash inflows	
Sale of old gasoline engine	$ 500
Savings on fuel over lifetime of truck	9,750
Total Cash Inflows	$10,250
Net Cash Flow (favorable)	$ 2,750

Thus, instead of showing a $2,250 loss, this cash flow analysis treats the investment in the gas engine as a sunk cost and shows a net savings of $2,750.

Actually Figure 3-11, the bookkeeper's approach, is not incorrect—just incomplete. There will be a book loss of $4,500—on sale of the gasoline engine. But if the diesel engine is not bought and the gasoline engine is kept, *there will still be an accounting charge to income for depreciation* on the gas engine, totalling $5,000.

The drawback to the bookkeeper's approach can be explained another way: the $5,000 paid for the gasoline engine is a sunk cost and can be ignored for purposes of decision making. It is not a cash item relating to this decision. Also, it can be ignored from an accounting point of view, because it will be a charge to the income statement no matter what decision is made: if the gasoline engine is scrapped, there will be a "loss on sales of fixed assets" charged to income; if the engine is kept, there will be depreciation expense. These outcomes are presented in Figure 3-13.

**Figure 3-13
Accounting
Results—Red
Ball Problems**

If gasoline engine is kept	
Depreciation Cost Total	$ 5,000
Cost of fuel over lifetime of truck	65,000
	$70,000
If diesel engine is purchased	
Loss on sale of old engine	
($5,000—$500)	$ 4,500
Depreciation of diesel engine	7,000
Installation cost	500
Cost of fuel over lifetime of truck	55,250
	$67,250
Difference	$ 2,750

To summarize, then, a sunk cost is the cost associated with a past decision. In an analysis of the merits of alternative courses of action, the relevant costs are those that will be affected by the decision at hand. These are costs that will be incurred after the decision is made. Since a sunk cost is a past event, it cannot be affected by an current decision and consequently is not a relevant cost.

This is not to say that accountants should not keep track of sunk costs that have been capitalized. They certainly should, and such costs should be written off over the proper period of time so that the firm's income statement will incorporate generally accepted and expected accounting procedures.

Some capitalized costs may even be written off or amortized according to units produced or machine-hours. As such, they will behave like variable costs. However, such costs are still reflections of a past decision and are not cash or out-of-pocket costs. The point here is that when evaluating current decision alternatives, one must remember that sunk costs are sunk and will not make any difference.

**DECISION
MAKING:
BREAKEVEN**

On the surface, calculating breakeven appears simple. Suppose that a computer rents for $5,000 per month. Variable costs for operating the computer center are $30/hour, and computer time is "worth" (or can be sold for) $80/hour. What is the breakeven point of operations?

In this instance, *breakeven point* refers to the number of hours per month that will leave the computer center with neither profits nor losses. The solution can be quickly found by analyzing contribution or by making a graphical analysis, as shown in Figures 3-14 and 3-15.

**Figure 3-14
Breakeven
Analysis of
Contribution**

Selling price	$80/hour
Variable costs	30
Contribution	$50/hour

$$\frac{\text{Fixed Cost}}{\text{Contribution/hour}} = \frac{\$5,000}{\$50} = 100 \text{ hours} = \text{Breakeven}$$

**Figure 3-15
Breakeven
Graphical
Analysis**

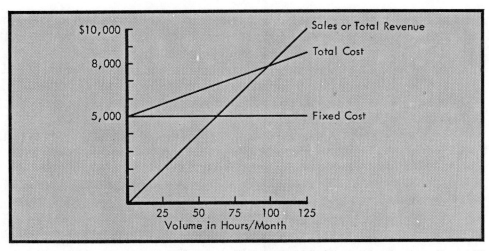

In the analysis of contribution, we find that each hour of operation will yield $50 toward covering fixed costs. Only 100 such hours are needed before all fixed costs are recovered. We can prove this calculation as follows:

Sales (at 100 hours)		$8,000
Less:		
Variable Costs	$3,000	
Fixed Costs	5,000	8,000
Profit (or Loss)		$ 0

These same relationships can be graphed as in Figure 3-15 to show the breakeven point. The steps are as follows:

1. Volume is typically shown on the horizontal axis. In this case the units of measure are hours/month.

2. Dollars are generally plotted on the vertical axis.

3. Fixed costs are plotted first. They are $5,000 for all levels of volume, so the fixed cost line is horizontal.

4. Variable costs at each level of volume are *added* to the fixed cost to give total costs. At 25 hours, variable costs are $750, so total costs are $5,750. At 50 hours, variable costs are $1,500, so total costs are $6,500.

5. Sales or revenues are then plotted for each level of volume. At 25 hours, sales are $2,000; at 50 hours, $4,000.

6. The point at which the sales line intersects the total cost line is the breakeven point. It is 100 hours.

The concept of breakeven is used in many manufacturing and service industries to express the interrelationships between sales price, volume, fixed costs, and variable costs. Study these other examples:

A chain of supermarkets uses breakeven calculations to help gauge the desirability of new store locations. Management estimates a store's costs for lease, utilities, rent, and manager and staff salaries at, say, $800,000 per year. The typical customer spends $2,000 per year, and the cost of a typical customer's purchases averages 80% of the selling price. Thus, the chain needs 2,000 customers to break even. (This supermarket measures volume by customers/year.)

A manufacturing company makes children's toys that sell for $2.00 and whose variable cost is $1.00/unit. Fixed costs are $250,000 per month. Their breakeven point is 250,000 units/month.

A hospital plans to build a new wing with 100 new beds. Fixed costs, including depreciation, will be $28,000 per week. The hospital rate/day is approximately $100, of which $50 goes to variable cost. Breakeven on the new facility is 80% occupancy.

Breakeven analysis can also be used to test the effect of a change in present operations. Any one or two of the variables can be increased or decreased to simulate a variety of situations. Here are five examples.

Legend:

FC —	Fixed Cost	FC & P —	Fixed Cost plus Target profit
TR —	Total Revenue	TC & P —	Total Cost plus Target profit
TC —	Total Cost (Fixed plus Variable)		

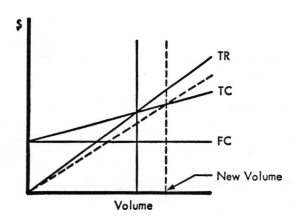

Volume

1. If we reduce our price 10%, what is our new breakeven volume? (Revenue per unit will decrease; volume is the unknown variable.) The diagonal dotted line represents the new revenue line, and where it crosses the Total Cost line is the new breakeven volume.

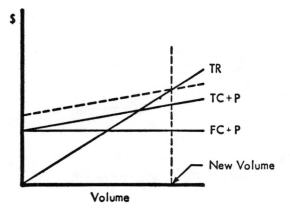

Volume

2. If we allocate another $50,000 to advertising, what increased volume must be stimulated to yield at least as much net profit as before? (Fixed costs will increase; volume is the unknown.) The new dotted Total Cost plus Target Profit line is higher than the old TC + P line by $50,000.

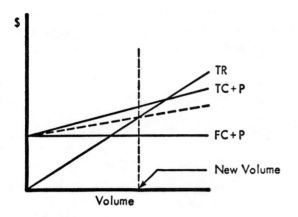

3. If we redesign the product and decrease the cost per unit, how much volume erosion can we have before profits will decrease? (Variable cost per unit decreases; volume is the unknown.)

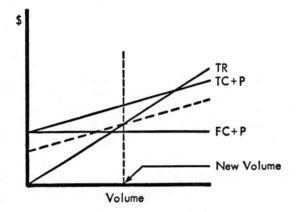

4. If a competitor enters our market and cuts our volume by 15%, what fixed cost reduction will be necessary to bring profits back to the previous level? (Volume is reduced; fixed cost is the unknown. Slope of the new TC + P line remains the same because the unit cost is unchanged.)

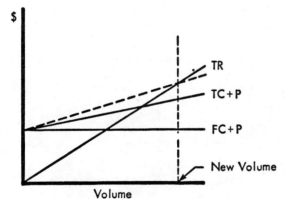

5. Though a price change is not feasible, we can increase our sales by 25% and our market share from 20 to 25% by redesigning our product to include higher cost material and quality standards. How much will be available for improved product quality if we wish to make at least our current profit? (Volume increase is given; the unknown is the increase in variable cost per unit.)

Note that breakeven analysis is often made in terms of zero profit. However, any level of profit can be incorporated in the analysis. If profit is a fixed dollar amount, as shown in the five examples, then it should be considered as a fixed cost. If it is defined as a set amount per unit sold, then the desired profit per unit would be one of the variable costs.

BREAKEVEN WITH MULTIPLE PRODUCTS

These simple examples belie a more complicated situation. We can explore the problem more fully by going back to Sunshine Manufacturing Company. What is its breakeven point?

A few moments of thought produces the remarkable conclusion that there are a great many breakeven points! By using the variable margin from Figure 3-3 we see that Sunshine will break even under several conditions:

Breakeven

	Model	Volume	Proof
	A	13,939	$33 margin × 13,939 units = $460,000
	B	0	-0-
or if:	A	0	-0-
	B	12,105	$38 margin × 12,105 units = $460,000
or if:	A	10,000	$33 margin × 10,000 units = $330,000
	B	3,421	$38 margin × 3,421 units = $130,000
			$460,000

or indeed many other combinations of volume.

Clearly, this multiplicity of answers is not what we had in mind when we tried to find *the* breakeven point for Sunshine. Does this mean that whenever there are multiple products or multiple services, it is not possible to find *the* breakeven point? Unfortunately, the answer is yes.

However, companies ordinarily make a compromise that allows them to calculate a single breakeven point. Study the illustration in Figure 3-16. With a projected volume of 20,000 and 5,000 units, respectively, Products A and B will yield $1,325,000 in sales revenue (step 1). At this volume, gross profit will be $850,000 (step 2) or 64% of sales (step 3). Since this analysis, in effect, says that each sales dollar provides 64¢ toward fixed costs, then the sales volume necessary to just cover the $460,000 of fixed cost is $718,750 (step 4).

Figure 3-16

SUNSHINE MANUFACTURING COMPANY
Breakeven Point

Step		A	B	Total
1.	Sales Price/Unit	$ 50	$ 65	
	× Volume	× 20,000	× 5,000	
	Total Estimated Sales	$ 1,000,000	$ 325,000	$ 1,325,000
2.	Sales Price/Unit	$ 50	$ 65	
	− Variable Cost	17	27	
	Gross Profit/Unit	33	38	
	× Volume	× 20,000	× 5,000	
	Total Gross Profit	660,000	190,000	850,000

3. $\dfrac{\$\ 850,000}{\$1,325,000} = 64\%$ Contribution/Sales Ratio

4. $\dfrac{460,000}{.64} = \$718,750$ Sales Volume Breakeven

Thus, the breakeven point for Sunshine Manufacturing is $718,750 of sales. Sales dollars become the units of measure for volume. The reader should be aware of the two key assumptions underlying this approach to breakeven:

1.   The sales "mix" is always assumed to be four of A to one of B.

2.   The gross profits are $33 and $38 for A and B, respectively.

If these assumptions become invalid, the breakeven point must be recalculated. Since most organizations are concerned with multiple products or services, these underlying assumptions are always present in an organization's breakeven figure.

DECISION MAKING: THE IMPACT OF TAXES

The effect of a particular decision on income taxes is a relevant consideration because taxes are out-of-pocket costs. Ordinarily, the taxing implications are easy to determine. If the effective total income tax rate (federal and state where applicable) is 52% then every $100 of additional savings or profits is worth $48 while every $100 of additional expenditures has a relevant cost of only $48. Some special tax problems related to purchase and sales of fixed assets cause more problems. We can illustrate them with the Red Ball problem previously introduced.

Assume that Red Ball's effective tax rate is 30%. A differential cash flow analysis is shown in Figure 3-17. Look at the effect of taxes. The cost of the new diesel engine (Item 1) is the same either before or after taxes—$7,000—because there are no immediate tax savings or payments when fixed assets are purchased. However, over the lifetime of the engine, $7,000 of depreciation expense will be charged to income, thus reducing taxable income by $7,000. As a result of this non-cash charge to income, $7,000 × 30% or $2,100 less taxes will be paid. While the depreciation expense is a non-cash item, the taxes saved by this depreciation are cash flow items and are therefore relevant savings (Item 7). These savings explain why depreciation expense is sometimes called a tax shield—depreciation saves $2,100 in

Figure 3-17 Cash Flow Analysis—Red Ball Problem

	Before tax basis	After tax basis
Tax Rate: 30%		
Differential cash outflows		
1. Cost of New Diesel Engine	$ 7,000	$ 7,000
2. Installation Cost	500	350
3. Tax savings foregone on depreciation of gasoline engine	0	1,500
	$ 7,500	$ 8,850
Differential cash inflows		
4. Sale of old gasoline engine	$ 500	$ 500
5. Tax savings on loss on sale of gasoline engine	0	1,350
6. Savings on fuel over lifetime of the truck	9,750	6,825
7. Tax savings on depreciation of diesel engine	0	2,100
	$10,250	$10,775
Differential cash flow	$ 2,750	$ 1,925

taxes that would otherwise have been paid in cash. Items 1 and 7 could have been combined or netted out, leaving a net cost of the new engine of $7,000 less $2,100 or $4,900; however, it is best to separate the two items for reasons discussed later. The effect on the differential cash flow would be the same.

The effective after-tax cash flow cost of installation (Item 2) is $350 or $500 × 70%. The installation expense reduces taxable income by $500 × 30% or $150—thus, the net cost is only $500 − $150 or $350. The same logic applies to the fuel savings (Item 6).

Items 3, 4, and 5 are related. When the old gasoline engine is sold for $500, there is a *book loss* of $4,500 ($5,000 cost less the $500 received). This book loss saves $4,500 × 30% or $1,350 of taxes that would otherwise be paid (Item 5). However, if the gasoline engine were kept, depreciation of $5,000 would have been taken over the lifetime of the gasoline engine. This $5,000 of depreciation would have saved $5,000 × 30% or $1,500 of tax (Item 3). The sale of the old engine yields $500. There is no tax penalty or savings (Item 4). Taking these items together, we see that by selling the old engine, Red Ball receives $500 cash plus a tax savings of $1,350 on its book loss—but it gives up future depreciation on the gasoline engine that would have saved $1,500 in taxes.

DECISION MAKING: SPECIAL CONSIDERATIONS

Semi-variable costs. Some costs are neither fixed nor variable. Sometimes costs increase by large amounts because of only a small increase in volume, as when a new employee is hired or production is extended to a second shift or a new machine is acquired. Sometimes costs will increase per unit because of special premiums: overtime labor or raw materials purchased at premium prices compared to the lower prices of long-term purchase contracts.

In most cases semi-variable costs can be handled by differential analysis: one looks at what the total costs will be if the action is not taken and then compares this result to the level of total costs if the action *is* taken. The differences can then be studied and the decision made. Cost analysis on a per-unit basis is generally not applicable when there are semi-variable costs.

Timing. "All costs are variable in the long run and fixed in the short." This old saying generalizes the behavior of costs over time. In the short run, many costs are fixed or are independent of volume—costs such as depreciation, management salaries, and certain other overheads. But in time even these costs change; plants can be closed or expanded, management and staff can be decreased or increased, and many overhead costs can also vary. A cost such as insurance on the plant seems fixed today, but after a long enough time, say three or four years, it becomes a cost that not only changes but is related to overall production capacity, because it is related to plant size.

For example, if you're trying to decide whether or not it is worthwhile to run a particular job on the computer this afternoon, you must consider almost all of the costs of the computer center as fixed, since management can do little to reduce them. On the other hand, if the job will be run each day for the next three years, then almost all of the costs can be considered variable, since management can adjust the operating costs of the data center to correspond to the workload. For example, employees can be hired or fired, or equipment can be expanded or reduced.

Clearly, in making a decision, one must first determine its time frame before analyzing costs, since the same cost can be fixed today and variable tomorrow. This axiom also implies that the relevant costs of a product or service can also vary with time. Pricing a special product with a three-month life cycle is much different from pricing a similar product with a three-year lifetime.

DECISION MAKING: OPPORTUNITY COSTS

Sometimes the relevant cost of an item has nothing at all to do with accounting costs but is instead the value of that item if it were used in the best possible manner by the organization. For example, the copper in our warehouse may have cost 30¢/lb., but if the current market value is now 70¢/lb., using it today in a product deprives us of the ability to use it and some other product or to resell it for 70¢. Clearly, the copper has a value of 70¢; we say that its *opportunity cost* is 70¢ if it is used in a product.

Another way of looking at opportunity costs is to go back to our discussion of the gasoline engine. We consider the cost of that gasoline engine to be sunk, not because the money for it has already been spent but because it has no alternative use—its opportunity value is zero.

Sometimes the relevant cost in a particular situation is a *contingency cost*. Raw material may be a variable cost—say $2.00/lb. for a particular item. But if a purchase contract specifies that we must purchase at least 100,000 lbs., then that raw material cost is not variable if we purchase less than that amount. The cost is variable only if we purchase more than 100,000 lbs. Labor in a particular skill class may cost $3.50/hour, but if a labor contract guarantees 80% of the base rate, the incremental and variable cost for that labor is really only $.70/hour throughout the time of the labor contract. If production is stopped, there is still an opportunity cost of $2.80 (80% × $3.50) per hour.

Suppose that the spoilage rate for a machine is 3% and a new machine is being considered which will reduce spoilage to 1%. The cost of the new machine is known. What is the "worth" or relevant value of the 2% savings? Ordinarily, the labor, material, and other variable costs of the product are lost when the product is spoiled. However, if the plant expects to operate at capacity during the lifetime of the new machine, then the relevant cost is these variable costs *plus* the lost contribution that would have been earned on the items that (if not spoiled) could otherwise have been sold. In this situation the relevant cost is the opportunity loss (lost contribution) on the unsold products plus the lost out-of-pocket costs.

Production capacity may have an opportunity cost. If a plant is operating well below capacity, any new business that will contribute to fixed costs, even though it doesn't necessarily cover full costs, will improve profits (or reduce loss). However, as the organization begins to reach capacity operation, any commitment of capacity to one project or customer means that some other project or product cannot be produced. At full capacity, the use of resources has an opportunity cost—the contribution that could be earned by the most profitable alternative. In such cases it is important to consider each alternative and its contribution per unit of capacity. For example, if Sunshine Manufacturing's capacity is limited by assembly capacity and the labor rate

**Figure 3-18
Contributions
Per Unit
of Capacity**

		Zingos	
		A	*B*
1.	Assembly cost/unit	$ 1.50	$ 4.00
2.	Labor rate/hour	2.00	2.00
3.	Assembly hours (1./2.)	.75 hrs.	2 hrs.
4.	Sales Price	$50.00	$65.00
5.	Variable Costs	17.00	27.00
6.	Contribution	$33.00	$38.00
7.	Contribution/Assembly Hour (6./3.)	$44.00/hr.	$19.00/hr.

in the assembly department is $2.00/hour, we can make the following analysis of contribution.

Thus, at capacity, Sunshine should encourage sales of Model A and discourage sales of Model B, because the *contribution per unit of capacity* made by A is more than double that of B.

COMMENTS ON TERMINOLOGY

Some managers use the terms *incremental, marginal, differential, variable,* and *direct* as if they all had the same meaning. They do not. While different organizations have adopted varying connotations for these terms, most executives accept the following definitions.

1. *Differential* costs compare one alternative with another. This difference may be the variation in costs between one production level and another for the same product, or perhaps the cost differences between one product and another. All costs need not be considered—only those affected by the decision.

2. *Marginal* costs are the additional costs of production or service *for one more unit.* The level of volume must be specified. For example, one might say "the marginal cost of product 12 at 85% of capacity is $37.95."

3. *Incremental* costs are similar to marginal costs but may be specified to cover a given number of additional units: "the incremental costs of 100 gallons is $112.50 per gallon between 10 and 15 thousand gallons of daily production."

4. *Variable* costs are those costs that vary directly with volume. They approximate but are not always the same as out-of-pocket costs.

5. *Direct* costs, strictly speaking, are only those costs that can readily be identified or measured by product. Allocated costs, whether fixed or variable, are excluded. Many people confuse variable costs and direct costs. Depreciation on a special machine may be direct to a product but not variable.

6. *Out-of-pocket* costs are those that must be paid in cash. Excluded are non-cash costs such as depreciation and deferred taxes.

TIPS ON PROBLEM SOLVING

One of the most important arts of decision making is to identify correctly the problem. Many times the analysis becomes hopelessly confused because of failure to clearly state the problem. Another common failure is to overlook the best alternative from the start. All problems involve alternatives. Failure to identify all feasible alternatives damns the analysis from the start.

It is important to segregate all cost and revenue elements of a problem according to the relative time of their occurrence. Relevant costs that occur at different times should always be separated rather than combined, because money has a time value. Techniques of analyzing present and future values are available. These techniques require, among other things, that all cash flows be segregated by time period (month-by-month or year-by-year). Present value techniques will be discussed further in Chapter 8, Evaluating Capital Expenditure.

Many decisions require evaluation of numerous alternatives. In these situations it is generally best to select one as the base or reference point and then to conduct a differential analysis between that base point and each alternative. Ordinarily, one selects the status quo or "do nothing" alternative as the reference point. The differential analysis of the alternative to drop Model B Zingos (Figure 3-9) is a good example. The status quo was the base point; from that, the changes in revenue and costs were measured.

Sometimes, there is no status quo alternative. For example, the decision to build a new service center in a particular location with a particular capacity may already have been made; the only remaining question is whether to lease or to buy. In this case, the cash flow costs for each alternative may be projected and evaluated. The alternative with the lowest net cost is then selected (non-economic factors being equal).

Or a hospital may have reached capacity and must expand in order to provide continuing levels of service to its growing community. Expansion can take place in stages of varying magnitudes: the hospital may plan one large expansion that will satisfy needs for 12 years or several smaller two-year projects that will gradually expand capacity. Incremental expansion is much more expensive but minimizes idle capacity and has lower initial cost. The hospital must expand and there is no status quo alternative; the remaining alternatives are mutually exclusive. Again, each alternative can be judged on the basis of total present value cost, since the revenues are assumed to be the same.

A business may be trying to decide whether to prolong the life of a product via certain design changes and market promotions or to replace it with a new product. A net present value profit analysis, comparing one alternative to the other, would provide the best comparison. One might also wish to consider keeping the old product *and* introducing the new one as well. There are thus three alternatives: Keep the old with modifications, scrap the old and introduce the new. In this case each alternative can be compared with the others, or the expected profits of each can be determined and the most profitable selected.

part two

planning and reviewing costs

INTRODUCTION The management process involves cycles of planning and reviewing costs. The cycles are of varying length, sometimes as short as a few hours, as might occur in a small job shop estimating and performing a job, but usually much longer. The stages are the same however. First costs are estimated during the planning stage, then as operations are carried out, actual costs are gathered and later compared with the estimates. This comparison is then used when planning again for the next period of time.

47

The first chapter in Part Two concerns budgeting, which is a cost planning process oriented toward organizational units such as departments, divisions, etc. The second chapter is on standard costing which is a cost planning process oriented toward products or services, or in other words, the output of an enterprise. Variances can be computed by products or, by regrouping the data, for operating departments and cost centers which may handle several products.

The third chapter on variable costing describes a system which separates variable costs from those that are fixed or mostly fixed. By doing this on a continual basis, rather than occasionally for specific decisions such as was described earlier in the chapter on Relevant Costs, management can monitor product line contribution to fixed costs.

The last chapter is a short one which shows how three cost system design choices result in eight possible types of systems. The intention is to pull it all together in a comprehensive framework, with illustrations of each type of cost system.

4

Preparing and Using Budgets

Many people think of a budget as an imposed constraint on spending. "We must stick to the budget" is a frequent remark that reflects this view. When seen this way, a budget is a management tool for reducing expenditures, or at least keeping them from rising. Or put another way, by setting a tight budget, management can run an efficient operation.

Though this view has some truth in it, it is narrow and fails to put the budget in the context of the overall managerial process. Though budgeting is part of that process, it is certainly not the total means by which management controls or influences the behavior of an organization.

In this chapter, we will take a broader view of budgeting while we examine what budgeting is, its purpose, how it should work and what some of the pitfalls are that may interfere with an effective process of budgeting.

WHAT IS A BUDGET?

First of all, a budget is a written plan for the operation of a business, stated in quantitative terms, for a specified future period of time. The quantitative terms are usually dollars, but often other measures of physical volume or activity, such as pounds or manhours, may be used.

As a plan, the budget represents the output or conclusion of a planning process. Hence the preparation of a budget should be viewed not just as a compilation of numbers, but as the quantitative interpretation of action plans. For example, pushing numbers around might result in a budget calling for 15% increase across the board. Such a budget might be impossible to implement because even a small increase in production would call for a second shift or overtime, both of which might be impossible within the budget constraints of a 15% increase overall. Clearly the budgeting process in this instance should start with an action plan which is then converted into dollars and a budget plan.

A budget is also a means of communicating the agreed upon plans, and a way of encouraging adherence to those plans. More will be said on these aspects later.

TYPES OF BUDGETS

There are three basic types of budgeting in business. They are:

1. Cash budgeting

2. Capital budgeting

3. Periodic budgeting

Cash budgeting is concerned with projecting cash inflows and outflows over some future period. *Capital budgeting* is concerned with the allocation of resources to capital projects, such as buildings, equipment or other programs which have benefits lasting more than one year. Capital budgeting will be examined in Part Three of this book. *Periodic budgeting*, which this chapter will discuss, is concerned with budgeting revenues and expenses for a business organization for a specified time period. Periodic revenue and expense budgets are often called operating budgets.

THE PURPOSE OF AN OPERATING BUDGET

An operating budget may include budgeted revenue and expenses, or just expenses alone. It is a statement of expected revenue and expenses for the budget period, and as such represents a plan of operation expressed in financial terms. It is important to note that the budgeting process being considered here involves the preparation of the budget as well as its use after preparation.

The value of the budgeting process arises in three ways:

1. The budgeting process supplies a discipline in planning. Operations must be examined and planned in detail if a budget is to be constructed.

2. The budget acts as a guide to subsequent actions and a way of communicating operating plans in financial terms. In addition an approved budget may grant authority to spend up to the amounts shown in the budget.

3. The adopted budget provides a basis of comparison for telling whether and how actual operations have deviated from the plan. As such the budget is an important part of the management control process.

CONDITIONS NECESSARY FOR EFFECTIVE BUDGETING

There are several organizational and operational conditions which must be obtained in order to have effective budgeting. Some of these are:

1. *Endorsement* by management

2. *Involvement* by participants

3. *Realism* in terms of expectations

4. *Appropriate Detail and Time Period* covered by the budget

5. *Coordination* of assumptions, efforts, and differences

6. *Communication* to responsible managers

Each of these conditions is discussed below.

Endorsement

For a budget to serve as a meaningful plan of operations and as a vehicle for management control, it must have the endorsement of the total management structure of an organization. If top management enthusiastically provides the leadership for the use of budgets, support of the whole organization will likely follow.

Involvement

In order for the budget to be accepted as a realistic and objective plan, it is necessary for the executives responsible for operating under the budget to be involved in the preparation of the budget. An effective means of preparing the expense portion of a budget is to have each responsibility center prepare its own budget, starting with the smallest center. These expenses are then built up by layers of responsibility. If the people operating under the budget are involved in its preparation and accept it as being reasonable, they will be more responsive to meeting the stated objectives.

Realism

A realistic budget is an objective appraisal of the operating expectations under the conditions assumed. To be realistic, it cannot be based on hopes which promote over-optimism or on fears which lead to pessimistic appraisals. If the budget is not realistic, it will not be accepted by those who must operate under it. If it is not accepted, it cannot provide an effective management planning and control system.

Appropriate Detail and Time Period

The time period for which a budget is prepared must be meaningful from an operational point of view. The shorter the time period the more detailed the budget. It is usually a waste of effort to prepare a three year budget in the same detail that is appropriate for a one year budget. Many companies will prepare detailed budgets for the next year and less detailed budgets for the two following years. Before the end of each year the next year's rough budget is filled out in detail and adjusted for new environmental conditions and operating forecasts. At the same time a new year is added to the rough budget extending two years out.

Coordination

One person, often called a budget director or director of planning, should coordinate the efforts of those persons involved in the budgetary process. Differences may arise between departments or functions which will have to be resolved in order to make an integrated budget. The budget coordinator can serve this role.

A coordinated budget will emphasize the inter-relationships which exist among the various parts of an organization and the necessity for these segments to plan for the future within the same assumed environmental framework.

Communication

After the budget has been prepared, it should receive positive approval from top management. This approval, and the budget, or at least relevant portions, should then be communicated to all those persons responsible for operating under the budget. Effective communication involves and explanation of the budget and positive, active use of the budget for managerial planning and control.

An effective budget, then must be *realistic* in terms of expectations, cover a specified time period with appropriate detail, have *endorsement* or commitment by management, be prepared by those *involved, coordinated* to assure planning under the same assumed conditions, and *communicated* to those responsible for planning and control.

PREPARATION OF THE BUDGET

In many organizations, the budget process will commence about six months prior to the year being budgeted. At this time, the budget coordinator will begin developing information about the environmental framework in which the budget will be set. This framework involves the economic, social, and, for some organizations, the political conditions under which the organization expects to operate. The framework specifications then should be communciated to those people who are responsible for preparing the several parts of the budget.

Projected Revenues

For most business organizations, the preparation of the operating budget starts with a projection of sales volume.This is often done both in terms of some measure of physical activity and in dollars. The estimate of physical activity is necessary in order for various operating departments to project expenses. The translation of the physical output into dollars is especially important in those situations where a change in prices or product mix is expected. The dual set of projections—dollars and physical activity—permits more careful evaluation of performance against plan by product, division, price, and volume.

With due consideration given to the environmental factors previously mentioned, revenue projections are also usually influenced by inputs from salesmen in the field, market researchers, economists, and others attuned to the market environment for the particular goods or services whose volumes are being projected. These projections may be backed up or factored by statistical or other analytical means of testing.

The revenue projection should be built up by responsibility centers, and the final plan should be agreed to by those responsible for producing the revenue. In addition to breakdowns by responsibility centers, such as product lines, divisions, and departments, revenues should be projected for useful time periods. For some businesses, this may be monthly; for others, if there are significant periodic variations in revenues, it may be useful to have daily or weekly projections. An illustrative revenue projection is presented in Exhibit 4-1.

It should be noted that different products or services within the same business may have different seasonal or growth revenue patterns. For example, the Kolb Distributing Company in the following illustration has a definite seasonal pattern for Product A and a possible seasonal pattern for Product B. The pattern of Product B partially offsets the Product A pattern. There is an apparent strong growth trend for the Service Department. However, the Service Department contributes a relatively small amount of the total revenues.

Exhibit 4-1

KOLB DISTRIBUTING COMPANY
Projected Revenue for the Year, 1970
(dollars in thousands)

	Product A		Product B		Service Dept.		Total
Month	Units	Dollars	Pounds	Dollars	Hours	Dollars	Dollars
January	1,000	2,000	2,000,000	300	660	3.3	2,303.3
February ...	1,200	2,400	2,000,000	300	630	3.2	2,703.2
March	1,200	2,400	2,000,000	300	660	3.3	2,703.3
April	1,400	2,800	1,800,000	270	680	3.4	3,073.4
May	1,500	3,000	1,800,000	270	700	3.5	3,273.5
June	1,600	3,200	1,500,000	225	800	4.0	3,429.0
July	1,400	2,800	1,800,000	270	800	4.0	3,074.0
August	1,400	2,800	1,800,000	270	800	4.0	3,074.0
September ..	1,200	2,400	2,000,000	300	810	4.1	2,704.1
October	1,200	2,400	2,000,000	300	810	4.1	2,704.1
November ..	1,000	2,000	2,000,000	300	820	4.1	2,304.1
December ..	1,000	2,000	2,000,000	300	820	4.1	2,304.1
Total	15,100	30,200	22,700,000	3,405	8,990	45.1	33,650.1

The aggregate revenue forecast for the Kolb Company should be supported by further breakdown specifying who is responsible for the origination of the revenue, e.g., by field salesmen, showroom salesmen, and various sales managers.

Projected Costs and Expenses

For a manufacturing business, the amount of factory costs incurred is related to the volume of production rather than to the volume of sales. Production volume is often related directly to sales volume, but not necessarily so. Inventory could be reduced to support a sales volume, or production could be geared to build up the level of finished goods inventory.

Expenses for non-manufacturing businesses or non-manufacturing activities of a manufacturing business are based on volume of activity, such as invoices prepared, cartons shipped, pounds processed, or on the strategic plans of management for items such as advertising and research and development.

Manufacturing Costs

Direct manufacturing cost estimates are based on the total projected production volume, which is related to sales volume and inventory changes. Each production department can estimate the amount of material, labor and other costs necessary to produce the projected volume of finished goods. A departmental manufacturing cost budget is illustrated in Exhibit 4-2

The departmental manufacturing cost budget illustrated in Exhibit 4-2 is based on the production of a single product. If more than one product passes through the same department, the volume of each of the different products must be taken into consideration. Where many items are processed through the same department, it is helpful if a common unit of measurement, such as weight or length, can be used.

Exhibit 4-2

PAYNE SEAT COMPANY
Sanding Department
Manufacturing Cost Budget
For the Year 1970

Month	Units	Materials	Labor	Overhead	Total
January	1,000	$ 4,000	$ 2,000	$ 1,500	$ 7,500
February	1,000	4,000	2,000	1,500	7,500
March	1,000	4,000	2,000	1,500	7,500
April	1,100	4,400	2,200	1,550	8,150
May	1,100	4,400	2,200	1,550	8,150
June	1,150	4,600	2,300	1,575	8,475
July	1,200	4,800	2,400	1,600	8,800
August	1,200	4,800	2,400	1,600	8,800
September	1,150	4,600	2,300	1,575	8,475
October	1,100	4,400	2,200	1,550	8,150
November	1,050	4,200	2,100	1,525	7,825
December	1,000	4,000	2,000	1,500	7,500
Total	13,050	$52,200	$26,100	$18,525	$96,825

Labor costs are based on standard costs per unit (if a standard cost system is used) multiplied by the projected costs per unit. If engineered standards are not used, the projected (or estimated) labor costs, in effect, become a standard.

Material costs are computed similarly to labor costs—by multiplying the projected volume to be used by the standard (or expected) materials price.

Overhead costs are projected based on itemizing the non-labor and material costs for each department or responsibility center. Some overhead costs such as rent, depreciation, and taxes are relatively fixed, within a given time period. Others, such as power, cleaning supplies, and fringe benefits may vary closely with units produced, direct labor hours or dollars, or some other input measure.

Non-Manufacturing Expenses

Expenses for non-manufacturing departments or businesses are related to some unit of measurement other than production, e.g., sales or strategic plans. An expense budget for these activities could be constructed similarly to the departmental manufacturing budget but without columns for materials and labor.

Projected Profit

After revenue and expense budgets have been built up by responsibility centers, they can be combined to show a projected income statement for the budget period, broken down by months or quarters. For a profit-seeking enterprise, this is the objective of the budgetary process—to plan for and deliver a satisfactory profit level given the prevailing environmental conditions for the budget period. Budgeting is also essential for a non-profit seeking organization in order to plan requests for revenue allocations and to plan and control expenses within given revenue volumes.

COMPARISON OF ACTUAL TO BUDGET

In order for the budget to serve as a control vehicle actual performance must be measured against budget. Actual revenues and expenses should be collected by the same categories used for budgeting. For effective control, performance reports should be prepared according to responsibility center and should show clearly those expenses which are controllable by the responsible person and those over which he has no control. Some reports show only the controllable expenses on the theory that if non-controllable expenses are listed, they may cause confusion on the part of the responsible manager.

A budget performance report is illustrated in Exhibit 4-3.

Exhibit 4-3

PAYNE SEAT COMPANY
Sanding Department
Overhead Performance
January, 1970

Item		Amount		Over (Under)	
No.	Name	Budget	Actual	Amount	Percent
Controllable					
1001	Indirect Labor	$ 500	$ 550	$ 50	10.0
2001	Maintenance	200	220	20	10.0
3001	Utilities	300	330	30	10.0
4001	Supplies	300	320	20	6.7
5001	Travel	75	-0-	(75)	(100.0)
Non-Controllable					
6001	Taxes	25	25	—	—
7001	Depreciation	100	100	—	—
	Total	$1,500	$1,545	$ 45	3.0

A complete budget performance report should include an explanation of the reason for the variances from budget and plans for initiating or completing corrective action, if necessary. This performance report should be reviewed regularly with the responsible persons involved. This review will emphasize the continued endorsement of the budget by management and will aid in communicating useful operating information up and down the management ladder.

Timely Revisions

The type of budgeting discussed so far can be described as "static" budgeting. Once a projected volume of activity, such as revenue or production, is established, variances are computed against the costs associated with this fixed projection. Because significant environmental changes may take place within a short period of time, consideration should be given to periodic budget revisions. These revisions could be monthly or quarterly for the remaining months or quarters of a year.

VARIABLE BUDGETS

Though the purpose and function of variable budgets are the same as fixed budgets, their preparation is sufficiently different to warrant a separate discussion.

Variable budgets may be effectively used in businesses or parts of organizations in which a change in the level of activity is expected to change the level of costs. With variable budgets different amounts of costs are budgeted for different levels of activity.

Purpose of Variable Budgets

A static or fixed budget is based on a single level of activity, often the level which, in management's judgment, is most likely to occur. In some cases, such as governmental operations, a budget is fixed as a result of fixed levels of revenue or appropriations. But, it is most unlikely that sales, or other measures of activity, will occur exactly as planned. Correspondingly, it is not likely that actual costs will amount exactly to planned costs. The static budget, however, provides no means of stating what costs should be if the level of activity is different from that which was planned originally. The use of a static budget as a control vehicle is therefore limited.

A variable budget, on the other hand, will indicate an estimate of what costs should be at various levels of activity and when the actual level of activity becomes known as a period passes, actual costs incurred can be measured against the planned costs for that level.

Preparation of a Variable Budget
Historical Data

The first step in preparing a variable budget is to collect historical data which will provide a basis for determining past relationships between the volume of activity and costs. These past relationships can usually serve as a basis for projecting future cost behavior.

Figure 4-1 illustrates graphically the behavior of direct labor cost in relation to pounds processed. As shown on this graph, apparently $360 of direct labor cost is incurred if the operation is open at all. No additional labor costs are required until a volume of 6,000 pounds is reached. Above a volume of 6,000 pounds, direct labor costs vary directly, $0.06 per pound, with pounds processed.

**Figure 4-1
Graphic Illustration
of Relationship
Between Costs and
Volume of Activity**

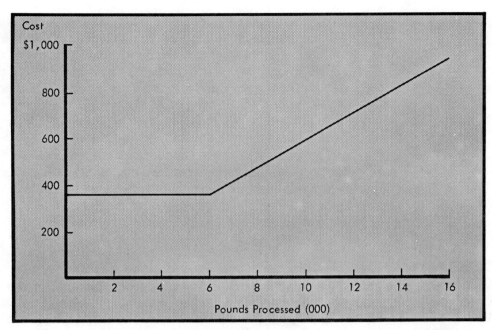

Measure of Activity

In order to measure the variability of costs, it is necessary to determine a measure of activity which has a close correlation with the work performed by the organization. The unit of measurement may be different for each department. The measurement unit can be dollar revenue, units produced, direct labor hours, pieces, pounds, or gallons. Some measures are based on *inputs* to a department, such as labor hours, whereas others are based on *outputs*, such as pounds processed. Figure 4-1 used an output measure, pounds processed, as the measure of activity.

The measure of activity should be that which has the highest degree of correlation with those costs which vary with the level of activity. It may be necessary to test the behavior of costs against several possible measures of activity to find the measure with the best correlation.

Range of Activity

For what levels of activity should a budget be prepared? Normally, a variable budget would be prepared only for those levels of activity which are probable, and not for all possible levels. The expected level of activity for the budget period should be projected. In addition, the probable range of activity should be projected. Thus, if the expected level of activity is projected as 100 percent, and the probable at plus or minus 20 percent, the variable budget would be designed for a range from 80 percent to 120 percent of the expected level.

The probable range of activity could be much wider for some organizations than for others. A power company, for example, would have a relatively narrow range. A local moving company, on the other hand, might have a relatively wide range because of the difficulty in projecting the number of people in the community who will move during the budget period.

It is necessary to specify the range of activity for which the variable budget is prepared. Costs which might be classified as fixed within an 80 to 120 percent range of expected volume, could change significantly if volume changes more than 20 percent. For example, additional space may have to be rented if volume increases more than 20 percent. At the other end, a minimum number of employees are always retained on the payroll. In Figure 4-1, if 12,000 pounds was the expected level of activity for the organization portrayed, the range of activity might be between 9,600 pounds (80 percent) to 14,000 pounds (120 percent). However, if the range of activity was much wider, or if the expected level of activity was 4,000 pounds, the cost variability of $0.06 per pound would not hold true.

Thus, in order to determine which costs are variable and which are fixed, for purposes of preparing a variable budget, it is necessary to work within a meaningful range of activity. For many organizations, if volume varies more than 20 percent plus or minus the expected level, a new budgeting effort is necessary.

DETERMINATION OF COST BEHAVIOR
Variable Costs

Within a selected range of activity, there are many costs which will vary proportionately, or almost so, with volume. These costs are classified as variable costs. For variable budgeting purposes, it is not necessary that a cost vary proportionately with volume at all levels—only at the levels within the selected range of activity—in order to be classified as a variable cost.

Fixed Costs

Some costs do not vary at all, or do not vary within a selected range of activity. These costs are referred to as fixed costs. Examples of fixed costs are rent, depreciation, and property taxes.

Semi-Variable Costs

How do you budget costs which vary, but do not vary in proportion to volume? There are different methods which may be used, four of which are discussed below. They are:

1.   Estimates for predetermined levels of activity.

2.   Arbitrary assignment of costs as either fixed or variable, based on their most dominant behavior.

3.   Breakdown by fixed and variable components.

4.   Graphic analysis.

Estimates at Predetermined Levels of Activity

Under this method, items of semi-variable costs such as maintenance costs are projected for predetermined levels of activity within the variable budget range. For example, predetermined ranges of 80, 90, 110, and 120 percent of expected volume could be used. Maintenance costs would then be budgeted at each of these levels based on estimated costs at these levels. The use of this method limits the variability of the budget because budget costs are calculated and can be compared with actual costs only at the predetermined levels. If actual volume were different from 80, 90, 110 and 120 percent of expected volume, budgeted costs would not be known exactly because costs at intermediate levels of activity would not necessarily follow a straight line pattern.

Assignment by Dominant Behavior

Another approach is to assign semi-variable costs to either the variable or fixed category according to its most dominant behavior. Thus, if a cost varies only by a small amount and not directly with volume, it is treated as a fixed cost. If a cost varies with a relatively high degree of variability but yet not in proportion to volume, it is treated as a variable cost.

Because this method is relatively simple and easy, it is widely used. However, it should be evident that this method is not exact and resort to it can affect the usefulness of the variable budget as a standard for cost behavior at various levels of activity within the range being used. The farther the results are from the expected level, the more distortion will be found.

Breakdown by Fixed and Variable Components

This method assumes that each item classified as a semi-variable cost can be broken down into variable and fixed elements. Thus, within a given range of activity a portion of a semi-variable cost would be considered as fixed while the remaining element would be assigned a proportional relationship to volume.

Under this method, an estimate is made of the level of each semi-variable cost at the likely upper and lower limits of the range of activity. For example:

	Pounds Processed	*Maintenance Costs*
Upper Limit	14,400	$2,432
Lower Limit	9,600	$2,288

In this example, as the number of pounds processed changed by 4,800 pounds, the maintenance costs changed by $144. Thus, the variable element of maintenance costs would be:

$$144 \div 4,800 \text{ pounds} = \$.03 \text{ per pound}$$

Having determined the cost per pound which is to be considered a variable cost, the fixed cost element can be determined.

	Upper Limit	*Lower Limit*
Total Maintenance Cost	$2,432	$2,288
Variable Costs		
14,400 pounds × $.03	432	
9,600 pounds × $.03		288
Fixed Cost	$2,000	$2,000

This method, using the upper and lower limits of the range of activity as a means of approximating the variable and fixed elements of cost items, is sometimes referred to as the "high-low method." Though it does not give precise cost relationships, it does give approximations which can be used at any level of activity within the given range.

Graphic Analysis

The high-low method of separating fixed and variable cost elements just described used only two points or levels of activity to make the variable cost determination. It is sometimes advantageous to use several points. These points are plotted on a chart with the vertical axis representing dollar cost and the horizontal axis representing the measure of activity (pounds in the example previously used). With the points plotted on a chart, a line of best fit can be drawn by visual inspection, or by more sophisticated statistical methods, such as a regression line based on the method of "least squares."[1] Figure 4-2 as an illustration of a graphic analysis of semi-variable costs.

Figure 4-2
Graphic Analysis
of Semi-Variable
Costs

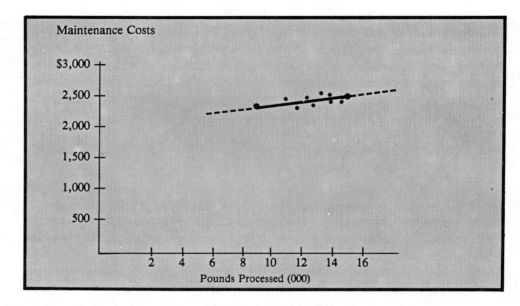

After the line of best fit has been plotted on a chart, the estimated cost can be read for any volume of activity. Thus, though a cost is not actually broken into its fixed and variable components, a total cost including both components is available for any level of activity within the range depicted. For computation without the graph, the point where the line intersects the vertical axis (here 2,000) and the slope of the line (here $.03 per pound) can be used to derive the total variable budget. Thus, $2,000 + .03 × pounds processed would give the variable budget for maintenance costs.

OBSERVATIONS
ON COST
BEHAVIOR

The following observations may be made about cost behavior:

1.   Total costs for an organization do not usually vary directly with volume of activity because some costs are fixed and some are semi-variable.

2.   Costs may not vary with volume at a constant rate. Some costs may vary in a step fashion, that is they may be constant for some increase in volume and then jump up with an additional increase. For example, with rising volume the cost of supervisors will be constant until one more must be hired. Other kinds of costs may vary continuously but at an increasing or decreasing rate. For instance, as working hours get longer, efficiency may go down, meaning that labor costs rise with volume but at an increasing rate. (Most companies recognize the

---

[1] This method is described in detail in most standard textbooks on statistics.

nonlinearity of cost changes but in constructing variable budgets conclude that a straight line is very much easier to use and represents a sufficiently close fit.)

3. Costs fluctuate as a result of three basic factors—volume, spending, and efficiency in utilization. For example, labor costs will usually increase as volume increases, as wage rates increase, or as labor is used inefficiently.

4. In comparing actual costs with budgeted costs, it is helpful to isolate those changes resulting from volume changes in order to make an appraisal of relative operating efficiency.

If a budget is to be used for performance evaluation as related to cost control, it must show what costs should be at various levels of activity. This, then, is the reason for variable budgets.

ILLUSTRATIVE VARIABLE BUDGET

Exhibit 4-4 shows a monthly budget for the processing department of the COD Delivery Company. Note that the costs for the processing department have been broken down into their fixed and variable elements, and that controllable and noncontrollable costs are shown separately.

Figure 4-4

COD DELIVERY COMPANY

Monthly Expense Budget
Processing Department

Measure of Activity—Pounds Processed

Cost item	Fixed cost per month	Variable cost per pound	9,600 80%	10,800 90%	12,000 100%	13,200 110%
			Range of activity			
Controllable Costs:						
Direct Labor	—	$ .06	$ 576	$ 648	$ 720	$ 792
Machine Rental	800	—	800	800	800	800
Supplies		.02	192	216	240	264
Maintenance	2,000	.03	2,288	2,324	2,360	2,396
Power	1,200	.01	1,296	1,308	1,320	1,332
Total	$4,000	$ .12	$5,152	$5,296	$5,440	$5,584
Non-Controllable Costs:						
Supervision	$ 700	—	$ 700	$ 700	$ 700	$ 700
Rent	300	—	300	300	300	300
Depreciation	800	—	800	800	800	800
Total	$1,800		$1,800	$1,800	$1,800	$1,800
Total Costs	$5,800	$ .12	$6,952	$7,096	$7,240	$7,384

Costs have been budgeted for selected levels of activity—80 to 110 percent of expected volume. With each cost item shown by fixed and variable elements, budget costs can be determined for various levels of activity between the selected levels. For example, if the actual level of activity for a month is 10,000 pounds, direct labor costs should be 10,000 × $.06 or $600. If the actual activity is 13,200 pounds, direct labor costs should be 13,200 × $.06 or $792.

ILLUSTRATIVE PERFORMANCE REPORT

Exhibit 4-5 shows a monthly performance report for the processing department of the COD Delivery Company for the month of March 1970. The expected level of activity was 12,000 pounds. Actual volume was 13,000 pounds. Using the budget shown in Exhibit 4-4, it is possible to determine the budgeted cost for each cost item at 13,000 pounds. For example, the budgeted cost for labor is 13,000 × $.06 or $780; actual labor cost was $788, so there was an unfavorable variance of $8. Again, the budget cost for maintenance is $2,000 (fixed) plus 13,000 pounds × $.03, or $2,390. Actual costs were $2,500, so there was an unfavorable variance of $110.

Exhibit 4-5

COD DELIVERY COMPANY

Monthly Performance Report
Processing Department

March, 1970

Measure of Activity—Pounds Processed
Budgeted Activity —12,000
Actual Activity   —13,000

Cost item	Actual cost	Budgeted cost	Variance $	Variance %	Remarks
Controllable Costs:					
Direct Labor	$ 788	$ 780	$ 8	1.0	
Machine Rental	800	800	—	—	
Supplies	270	260	10	3.8	
Maintenance	2,500	2,390	110	4.6	
Power	1,324	1,330	(6)	(0.5)	
Total	$5,682	$5,560	$122	2.2	
Non-Controllable Costs:					
Supervision	$ 740	$ 700	$ 40	5.7	
Rent	300	300	—	—	
Depreciation	800	800	—	—	
Total	$1,840	$1,800	$ 40	2.0	
Total Costs	$7,522	$7,360	$162	2.2	

With a properly constructed variable budget, it is possible to determine what costs should be at any volume within the selected range of activity. Thus, poor performance cannot be blamed on changes in volume. Conversely, a decrease in volume will not make a department manager look good by showing favorable cost variances due in part to a change in volume.

ISSUES IN IMPLEMENTING THE BUDGETING PROCESS

As described in the previous sections, the process of budgeting sounds quite straight forward. However, its implementations is not as easy as it sounds. There are several critical issues whose handling will determine whether the budgeting process is effective: bottom up vs. top down, realism vs. control, and budget revision.

Bottom Up vs. Top Down Budgeting

With top down budgeting higher levels of management set the budget for the lower levels. It is a way of saying, "Here's what we want you fellows to do." With bottom up budgeting, on the other hand, the lower levels say, "Here's what we think we can do."

They each have advantages and disadvantages and most systems usually end up trying to achieve a good blend of the two. Bottom up budgeting, in which each level participates in setting its own budget goals, is most likely to generate commitment to meeting those goals. But those goals may be too easy or may not match the company's overall strategic objectives in such areas as profit level or market penetration. Top down budgeting insures that budgets will be acceptable to higher management but lack of commitment by those lower down who are responsible for achieving the budget targets may endanger the plan's success.

Clearly a good budgeting system must have some of each. Sometimes this is done by working in stages as follows:

1. Top management assesses the market and business environment and sets a strategic framework including level of volume and profit for the various product lines.

2. With these general targets, operating management works on detailed plans and costs, arriving at a proposed budget.

3. Through discussion and negotiation agreement is reached on a budget that is deemed to be both achievable and appropriate for the company's overall strategic objectives.

Realism vs. Control

Budgeting is both a planning device and part of the control system. The two can work at cross purposes. For planning one wants realistic and reliable forecasts yet the control system may not encourage this. If the control system compares actual results with forecasted results, and penalizes managers in some way when actual results fall short of what was forecasted, the next time around the manager whose performance is being measured will naturally try to avoid any penalty by forecasting goals that he is not likely to miss. These forecasts may not be the best forecasts for planning purposes.

There is no easy solution to this conflict. The budget certainly has a place in both the planning and control systems. Excessive reliance can be mitigated; to some extent higher management can "second guess" lower management's projections, and to some extent variances from budget should be interpreted in the light of whatever uncontrollable influences were present.

The same sort of conflict also exists in the budget approval process. If one year's proposed budget is cut, the next year's proposed budget is likely to have a cushion so that after being cut it will still be satisfactory. Recognizing this, the next cut is likely to be deeper. This game goes on in government as well as business. It probably can never be completely eliminated, but smart budget makers and approvers will know it is there and try to keep its distortions to a minimum.

Budget Revision

In an annual budget cycle, conditions may change, so that before the end of the budget year, the budget represents an unrealistic plan. Should the budget be revised?

Some say, "Of course it should," for an unrealistic budget does more harm than good. Others say, "no it should not," because a budget that is changed too easily and frequently is a confusing guide and has little discipline. And of course to some extent both views are right.

If a budget is revised, it should be done with the same analytical process that provided the basis for the original budget. Otherwise, budget revisions made in one department would cause that budget to wander out of coordination with other units in the company or overall company strategy.

Some companies stick with the original budget but ask department or division managers to forecast each month how they now think they will do for the rest of the year in comparison to the budget. These forecasts then become the subject of discussion and if accepted, a sort of revised budget for control purposes.

CONTINGENCY PLANNING

It is highly unlikely that actual revenues and expenses will agree with the amounts budgeted. Yet, many companies expect the profit as budgeted to be delivered regardless of what happens to the level of revenues. Contingency planning can be very useful in managing to achieve the desired profit level.

Contingency planning is often associated with "what do we do if things go bad." It can be just as useful when things go better than expected. Thus, contingency planning, as described here, is planning the actions to be taken when actual events do not correspond with the assumptions used in preparing the budget.

If sales do not materialize as budgeted, a contingency plan, prepared at the same time as the budget, would include the steps to be taken to reach the desired profit level. These steps could include more expenditures in the marketing or sales area or the reduction of "managed expenses" such as research and development, training, maintenance, and travel.

One of the essential ingredients in contingency planning is identifying a "trigger" point which would signal the necessity to implement a contingency plan. The trigger point could be an economic indicator, the level of incoming orders, a strike at a competitor's plant, or anything different from the assumed conditions used in the budget.

The preparation of contingency plans during the budget process means that the plans can be prepared on a more rational basis than waiting until something happens during the operating period which requires fast action. Fast action, without prior planning, is often done on a more emotional basis and is less apt to be rational.

Contingency plans are of little benefit unless they are executed when the "trigger" is pulled. Many companies prepare plans but are hesitant to implement them until it is too late to realize the intended results.

SUMMARY

In this chapter we have discussed budgeting, which is really a planning and review process. Six conditions were described as necessary for effective budgeting:

1. Endorsement

2. Involvement

3. Realism

4. Appropriate Detail and Time Period

5. Coordination

6. Communication

The process of preparing a budget, both a static budget and a variable budget were described and illustrated. Three issues were examined whose resolution was crucial to the effectiveness of the budgeting process:

1. The need for balance between bottom up and top down budgeting.

2. The conflict between the need for realistic and reliable numbers for planning and the use of budget comparisons for performance evaluation.

3. The question of when and how to revise a budget.

A final section discussed contingency planning as a means of managing when assumed conditions in the budget are changed.

5

Standard Costing Systems

Standard costing systems serve many of the same functions as operating budgets. Budgets are plans of operation stated in financial terms. In standard costing systems the planned cost of a product is called its standard cost. Preparing budgets and standard product costs are important parts of planning, and comparing the actual results with budgets and standards helps management to see whether the plan is being followed.

There are, however, some important differences between standard costs and budgets. Whereas budgets are usually made for an organizational unit, standard costs are usually prepared for a unit of production or service output. For example, the standard cost for a water pump would include the standard cost of several castings. The castings department would have an annual budget for its operations and might well cast parts for other products besides the water pump.

Standard costs, then, represent planned product costs and, like budgets, enable actual costs to be compared with the plan. The difference between actual cost and standard cost is called *variance*. This chapter will explain how standard costs are computed and how several kinds of variances can be developed that will give management useful information about the operation.

In addition to providing variance information, standard cost systems also have the benefit of simplifying a firm's accounting for inventories. Since inventory is valued at standard cost, an item is always carried at the same cost, regardless of when it was made or how much the material or labor put into it actually cost. The inventory value per item changes only when the standards are changed.

Installation of standard costing systems may be costly, since an investment of time and effort is usually required to establish the standard costs and to incorporate them in the accounting system. In addition, standards must be kept up to date and new standards computed for each new product. Where standard costing systems are used, however, these installation and maintenance costs are more than offset by the benefits from simpler inventory accounting and valuable control information.

Let us see in some detail how a standard costing system works. The first example describes a simple system involving one product and one cost center. The second example makes the second production stage a separate cost center, and the third example explains how several products are handled.

EXAMPLE 1: STANDARD COSTING WITH ONE PRODUCT, ONE COST CENTER

The company in our first example produces drumcaps in two production steps: machining and assembly. In this first example, both machining and assembly are treated as parts of a single cost center.

The first step in setting up a standard cost system is to construct a *standard cost sheet* for each item to be produced. A standard cost sheet is reproduced as Exhibit 5-1.[1] Such a sheet will show

1.   The standard amounts of direct materials per unit of output, in this case per 100 drumcaps, and the standard cost of that material.

2.   The standard hours of direct labor per 100 drumcaps and the standard rate.

3.   The amount of overhead allocated to the 100 drumcaps using the preset overhead rate for the single cost center.

The standard cost sheet is usually prepared or revised once a year for continuing products and throughout the year whenever new products are developed. Drumcaps are a standard item so this standard cost sheet was prepared in November.

In January the plant produced 10,000 drumcaps so $1,600 was added to the finished goods inventory. Half of these were sold, so cost of goods sold (at standard) was $800, leaving $800 in the finished goods inventory at the end of the month. There is no work-in-process at month end.

At this point, we have no information on what our actual costs were for the month. So the accountants go to work and discover the following information:

---

[1] It may be noticed that this standard cost sheet looks very much like a job cost sheet, an example of which is shown in Chapter 2.

Exhibit 5-1
Standard Cost
Sheet

```
                        Standard Cost Sheet


Drumcaps:     cost per 100                      1/1/70


Material:

          20 ft. #36 rod at $.18/ft.        $3.60
          100 washers at 1.00/m               .10
          100 nuts at 3.00/m                  .30

          Total Material                              $ 4.00


Labor:

          Machining 1.5 hrs. @ $4.00        $6.00
          Assembly 1.0 hrs. @ $2.00          2.00

                                                      $ 8.00

Overhead @ 50% direct labor                             4.00


          Total Manufacturing Cost (per 100)          $16.00
```

1. We used 2,050 feet of #36 rod.

2. We used 10,100 washers.

3. We used 10,300 nuts.

4. Machinists worked 140 hours.

5. Assembly workers worked 115 hours.

6. Manufacturing overhead was $425.

7. Prices paid for material and wage rates paid the workers were the same as the set standards.

A lightning calculation tells us that what we actually used and spent was not quite what it would have been had we exactly met the standards. The accountant would usually handle these discrepancies by adding to work-in-process $369 for the #36 rod used (2,050 × $.18) and transferring $360 from work-in-process to finished goods. This transaction leaves $9 in work-in-process, which should be at zero since there is actually no inventory there. The accountant then transfers the $9 to a material variance account, leaving zero in work-in-process. Finished goods and cost of goods sold stay at standard cost per 100 drumcaps.

The accountant then follows the same procedure with the other five items and ends up with the following items in variance accounts:

Item	Actual	Standard		Variance
Material: #36 rods	$369.00	$360.00		$ 9.00 (50 extra feet)
Material: washers	10.10	10.00		.10 (100 extra washers)
Material: nuts	30.90	30.00		.90 (300 extra nuts)
Machining labor	560.00	600.00	cr.	40.00 (10 hrs. less labor)
Assembly labor	230.00	200.00		30.00 (15 hrs. extra labor)
Overhead	425.00	400.00		25.00 ($25 extra overhead)

All variance accounts except the machining labor variance account have left-hand (debit) entries. The machining labor account has a right-hand (credit) entry. All left-hand variances are "unfavorable," sometimes also called "negative" variances because they cause a decrease in profit. The machining labor, then, is a "favorable" or "positive" variance. Unless he had good reason to do otherwise, the accountant would finish his work on variances for the month by closing them to the profit and loss account for the period. The monthly income statement which he has drawn up for management shows them as separate entries (See Exhibit 5-2.) Alternatively, he might have combined them with manufacturing overhead and/or cost of goods sold. Whichever way he handles it, management would always have in the records the amounts of the individual variances, which could be discussed with the persons responsible.

**Exhibit 5-2
Income
Statement**

Sales (5,000 drumcaps)		$1,000.00
Standard Cost of Goods Sold		800.00
Standard Gross Margin		$ 200.00
Variances		
Material—rod	($ 9.00)	
Material—washers	(.10)	
Material—nuts	(.90)	
Labor—machining	40.00	
Labor—assembly	(30.00)	
Overhead	(25.00)	
Net Variances		($ 25.00)
Actual Gross Margin		$ 175.00

**EXAMPLE II:
STANDARD
COSTING: ONE
PRODUCT, TWO
DEPARTMENTS**

In the previous example the factory was treated as one large department with one plant-wide overhead rate. Let us now separate the plant into two departments, machining and assembly, to see how standard costing would apply to the two cost centers.

The total budgeted plant overhead of $400 a month must now be reexamined and distributed to the departments. In this case $300 goes to machining and $100 to assembly. The machining department is assigned more overhead because it uses a greater amount of equipment.[2] Since the planned volume of work for each department is 10,000 drumcaps, the overhead works out to $3 per 100 drumcaps in the machining department and $1 per 100 drumcaps in the assembly department.

With this division of budgeted overhead between the two departments and the standards shown in the standard cost sheet, the resulting standard cost system is illustrated by the T accounts shown in Exhibit 5-3 with descriptions of the 14 transactions used to apply costs and develop variances. Explanations of the numbered transactions follow.

1. 2,050 feet of rod were taken from the raw material inventory account and added to Work-in-Process—Machining Department ($369).

2. Machinists worked 140 hours on the rods; $560 is transferred from direct labor payroll to W.I.P. Machining.

3. Overhead is added to W.I.P. Machining on the basis fo $3 per hundred drumcaps machined ($300).

4. The 10,000 machined drumcaps are transferred at standard cost to the assembly department. The standard cost of each hundred units is $3.60 (material) plus $6 (labor) plus $3 (overhead), or $21.60. One hundred of these lots have a total standard cost of $1,260.

5. 10,100 washers are transferred to W.I.P. Assembly ($10.10).

6. 10,300 nuts are transferred to W.I.P. Assembly ($30.90).

7. The assemblers worked 115 hours on assembly ($230).

8. Overhead is added to W.I.P. Assembly at $1 per hundred drumcaps assembled ($100).

9. 10,000 completed drumcaps are transferred to Finished Goods ($1,600).

10. 5,000 drumcaps are sold; cost of goods sold at standard cost is $800.

---

[2] Chapter 2. "Organizing the Cost Information," contains a fuller discussion of the process by which overhead is distributed to various departments.

At this point, the end of the month, inventory is taken and no drumcaps are found to be in process. Any balances in the W.I.P. accounts then represent variances from standard and must be transferred to variance accounts.

11. The $31 credit balances in W.I.P. Machining is transferred to Material Variance, debit $9, and Labor Variance, credit $40.

12. The debit balance of $31 in W.I.P. Assembly is transferred to Material Variance, debit $1, and Labor Variance, debit $30.

13. Actual overhead is $315 in the machining department (some allocated, some direct) and $110 in the assembly department. The other half of this transaction consists of credits to a number of accounts, such as Cash, Accounts Payable, Accrued Payroll, and Accumulated Depreciation.

14. Since the two overhead accounts are temporary accounts used during the accounting period, they are closed out and their balances are transferred to Overhead Variance ($15 and $10).

**Exhibit 5-3
Standard Costing:
T Accounts**

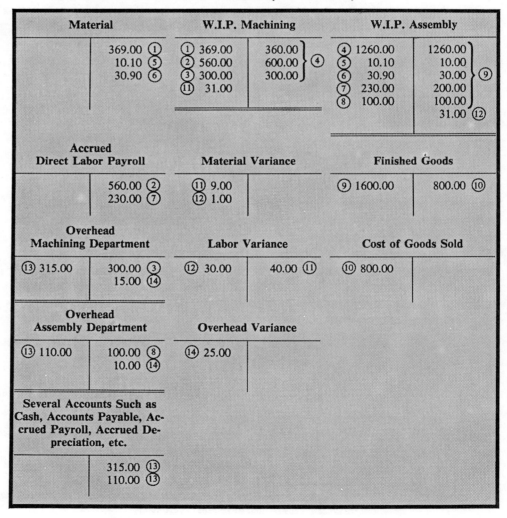

VARIANCE ANALYSIS

After these transactions are recorded, management has in its records the amounts of the several variances and might call for a production report such as the one shown in Exhibit 5-4.

Several facts should be noted about this report. The report says that production for the month was 10,000 drumcaps, which has a standard cost of $1,600. Column one shows the standard cost of the actual drumcaps produced, by type of expense. The second column shows what the actual costs were, and the third column shows the variance. The last column gives the variance as a percent of standard cost. The dollar size of a variance is important, but the percent of deviation is also worth noting because it can show whether the variance is a relatively small random deviation or whether it is significant.

**Exhibit 5-4
January
Production
Report**

	Standard cost	Actual cost	Variance	% of std. cost
Machining Dept.				
Direct Material	$ 360	$ 369	$ 9.00 (unfavorable)	2.5
Direct Labor	600	560	40.00 (favorable)	6.7
Overhead	300	315	15.00 (unfavorable)	5.0
	$1,260	$1,244	$16.00	
Assembly Dept.				
Direct Material	$ 40	$ 41	$ 1.00 (unfavorable)	2.5
Direct Labor	200	230	30.00 (unfavorable)	15.0
Overhead	100	110	10.00 (unfavorable)	10.0
	$ 340	$ 381	$41.00 (unfavorable)	
Total	$1,600	$1,625	$25.00 (unfavorable)	

Production for the Month: 10,000 Drumcaps
Standard Cost of Actual Volume: $1,600.00
Variances by Department:

EXAMPLE III: STANDARD COSTING, MULTIPLE PRODUCTS

Most companies produce more than one product. When such is the case, keeping track of actual costs for each product would require a job costing system similar to the one described in Chapter 2. Actual costs would be recorded on a job sheet and variances would be available for each job or product.

The question of whether or not to record costs by product did not arise in the first two examples, because only one product was made—drumcaps. All costs were automatically the costs of that product.

A standard costing system, however, does not have to record actual costs by product. A much simpler and frequently used system records costs and develops variances by type of input, such as labor or material, but not by each individual job or product.

For example, suppose that after the #36 rod entered the machining department it was made into five different products. During the month we could debit the machining department for the actual amount of rod used for all products and credit the department for the standard material content of the units actually sent on to the assembly department. At the end of the month, after being adjusted for any inventory change in the department, the material variance will be the difference between the actual input and the standard material content of all units transferred out. The variance will pertain to the whole department, and we would have no information about which products caused it. If it were important to relate the variance to the products, we would have to record actual amounts on job sheets. However, if departmental variance is enough information, much detailed record-keeping can be avoided.

Direct labor costs can be handled the same way. Actual total labor costs in a department are often easily available from payroll records. The difference between the actual direct labor for the month and the standard direct labor content of units transferred out will be the monthly direct labor variance. Again, we will not know which product caused the variance.

With multiple products, it is likely that overhead would be applied using direct labor as a base rather than units produced. Direct labor is used because the several products may be quite different and require different amounts of effort to produce. Under these circumstances, the overhead required would be more closely related to direct labor used than to numbers of units produced. The labor base can be either the number of hours or the number of dollars of direct labor "contained" in the units actually processed. Using drumcaps production as an example and applying overhead on the basis of standard labor-hours, we reach the following results.

1. 10,000 machined drumcaps have a standard labor content of 150 hours. Since overhead in the machining department is expected to be $300, the rate of application would be $2 of overhead per standard labor-hour.

2. In assembly the standard assembly labor content of 10,000 drumcaps is 100 hours, so the rate used to apply the expected $100 of overhead would be $1 per standard direct labor-hour.[3]

There are other reasons why it may be easier and fairer to apply overhead on the basis of labor rather than production units. One is that the output units from a particular department may not be the same as the end product units. In the early stages of production, the units may be pounds and only in the later stages become identifiable end products. In these cases, labor content is a base common to all products, and it is often easier to establish an expected relationship between overhead and direct labor.

The variances we have discussed thus far have been quantity variances. Material prices or labor rates have not entered the picture. Price and rate variances will be discussed in the next section.

---

[3] Note that the example applies overhead on the basis of *standard* direct labor-hours rather than *actual* labor-hours. Most systems work this way, although it is possible to use actual hours as a base. More will be said about this later.

PRICE AND
RATE VARIANCES

When a standard cost for a product is established and laid out on a standard cost sheet, both standard quantities and prices are set. We have seen how quantity variances can result from differences between actual and standard quantities. Actual prices and rates may also differ from standard, resulting in price and rate variances.

Theoretically two sequences can be used to compute price and quantity variances. The diagram below helps to explain the alternatives.

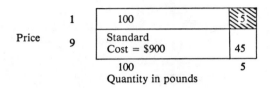

The standard cost per completed unit includes 100 pounds of raw material at $9.00 a pound or a total of $900 per unit of output. Actual usage was 105 pounds and the actual price was $10.00 a pound for a total cost of $1,050, or $150 over the standard cost. There is clearly both a price and a quantity variance. If we compute the price variance first, it is $105.00 (105 pounds times $1.00 increase in price.) The usage variance is then $45. If we compute the usage variance first, it is 5 lbs. times $10. The price variance is then $100. The question is whether the shaded $5 area is to be considered part of the price variance or part of the usage variance.

Customary practice almost always puts the $5 with the price variance. The price variance, therefore, would be identified first using actual quantity. Computation of the quantity variance will then use standard price. Labor rate variances are also identified first in virtually every case.

Material price variances may be developed when the material is put into production, or they may be developed when the material is purchased. The latter method allows raw material inventory to be kept at standard price per unit, which greatly simplifies the accounting system, since every unit of an item in inventory will have the same cost attached to it regardless of purchase price. However, in companies that purchase large amounts of raw material at irregular intervals and at widely fluctuating prices, this method may produce large favorable or unfavorable price variances that distort the income statement for the period. Purchase of six months supply of copper on December 30th might produce a price variance that would distort the year's results. Furthermore, the external accountants may worry that a favorable price variance on material purchased but not used will show a "profit" before the income has actually been realized. However, in most businesses significant distortions are rare, and it generally turns out to be easier to develop the material price variance at the time of purchase.

To carry this out, the standard cost of the amount of material purchased is added to Raw Material Inventory, and the difference between the actual and the standard costs is added to or deducted from a purchase price variance account. From then on, the raw material is always handled at the standard cost per unit.

Since labor is not carried in inventory by itself, purchase and usage occur at the same time. A standard rate for each operation is noted on the standard cost sheet, and if the actual rate is different, the difference is entered in a labor rate variance account at the time that the labor cost is applied to inventory.

OVERHEAD VARIANCE

Meaningful overhead variances are more difficult to develop than material and direct labor variances. While we can assume with some validity that material and direct labor costs will vary directly with volume, we cannot reasonably assume that overhead will do so. The standard for material and labor is a set amount per unit produced. If volume is above or below the level anticipated at the beginning of the year, the standard material and labor content will be correspondingly above or below the expected level, and the assumption is that actual material and labor costs will follow the standard amounts. In practice this is generally true for material, but with increasingly restrictive labor contracts, labor is becoming more of a fixed cost that does not easily vary with small changes in volume. Nevertheless, most cost systems incorporate the assumption that direct labor is variable, leaving it to those who interpret the variances to decide the extent to which the assumption is correct.

Manufacturing overhead, however, is generally assumed to be a mixture of fixed and variable costs. Some costs such as depreciation are known to be fixed, while others such as indirect labor and supplies may be largely variable. One can see that costs that are fixed in total will not be the same per unit produced if production volume varies. Thus, if overhead variances are to contain a useful message, there must be a way for variances to recognize that some overhead costs will remain fixed while others will vary with volume.

This recognition is granted in an overhead budget that specifies the expected level of overhead expense at various volume levels. The process is essentially the same as that described earlier in the section on variable budgets in Chapter 4.

Using the drumcap machining department, let us follow the sequence of steps.

1.   At the beginning of the year an estimate is made of the volume of production that the department is likely to have each month. In this case it is 10,000 drumcaps with a standard content of 150 hours of direct labor. This figure is often called standard volume.

2.   An estimate is also made of the amount of manufacturing overhead that the department will incur at the standard level of production. In this case it is $300 a month.

3.   From these figures we know that the standard overhead rate will be $2 per standard direct labor-hour. This figure is also known as the *overhead absorption rate* since work-in-process absorbs $2 of overhead

for each standard hour of direct labor contained in units transferred out.

4. Knowing that volume may not be exactly as predicted, we establish a *variable overhead budget*, which says how much overhead we think will be incurred at volumes other than standard. This estimate can be made examining past records to see how much actually was incurred at different volumes, or it can be done by asking people directly involved how much would be spent if volume were 10% over or under the standard volume.

Exhibit 5-5 shows a graph depicting the overhead absorption line ($2 per standard direct labor-hour) and the budget line. In this case the budget line shows that $240 of the $300 is fixed, and a rate of $.40 per standard direct labor-hour reflects the variable portion of overhead. Since the budget may not hold for volumes that vary greatly from standard volume, the budget line is dotted for low and high volumes.

Exhibit 5-5
Overhead
Budget for
Machining
Department

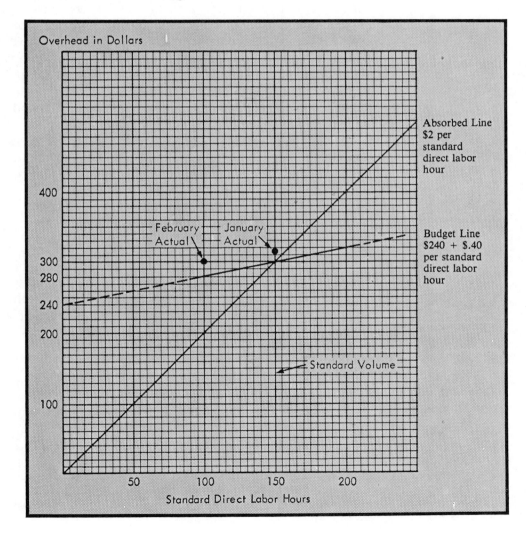

In the month of January the 10,000 drumcaps that were machined contained 150 standard direct labor-hours. Production was exactly at standard volume. The dot represents actual overhead at $315. The $15 overhead variance is represented by the vertical distance between the "actual" point and the point below it on the absorption line. In this case, that point is where the two lines cross since production was at standard volume.

Suppose production declines in February to 100 standard labor-hours. Absorbed overhead will be $200 (100 hours times $2 per hour). And let us also suppose that actual overhead is $300, marked by the other dot. The overhead variance shown in the accounting records will be $100 negative or unfavorable (absorbed overhead of $200 minus actual overhead of $300).

A look at the graph tells us that overhead was only $20 above the budgeted amount for that level of production, so the negative variance of $100 may be a bit misleading. At the level of 100 standard labor-hours of production, we expected to have $80 negative overhead variance; the other $20 was not anticipated. The $80 is called *volume variance*; the $20 is called *overhead spending variance* or *budget variance*. In this way the total overhead variance is broken into two components: the volume variance, which is caused by volume being below or above standard volume, and the spending variance, which is the difference between actual overhead and the amount budgeted at actual volume. As can be seen from the graph, the two variances add up to the total overhead variance. If actual overhead had been $260, the spending variance would have been a favorable $20, and the unfavorable volume variance of $80 combined with the favorable $20 spending variance would have netted out to a total variance of $60, unfavorable ($200-$260).

Expressed as formulas, the three overhead variances are computed as follows:

Volume variance = Absorbed minus Budgeted
Spending variance = Budgeted minus Actual
Total variance = Absorbed minus Actual
and
Total variance = Volume variance plus Spending variance.

Let us review ten possible combinations of overhead spending and volume variances and see how they are represented on the graph. Exhibit 5-6 shows ten dots, each representing a condition of volume of activity and actual overhead. The variances that would result are:

Dot No.	Activity	Volume variance	Spending variance	Net or total variance
1	Below Standard Volume	Negative	Negative	Negative
2	Below Standard Volume	Negative	Zero	Negative
3	Below Standard Volume	Negative	Positive	Negative
4	Below Standard Volume	Negative	Positive	Zero
5	Below Standard Volume	Negative	Positive	Positive
6	Above Standard Volume	Positive	Negative	Negative
7	Above Standard Volume	Positive	Negative	Zero
8	Above Standard Volume	Positive	Negative	Positive
9	Above Standard Volume	Positive	Zero	Positive
10	Above Standard Volume	Positive	Positive	Positive

Notice that the volume variance is always negative when actual volume is below standard, and positive when volume is above standard. This relationship says, in effect, that if actual overhead is as it was budgeted to be (zero spending variance), then we would expect a positive total variance when volume is above standard, and of course that total variance would be entirely volume variance. Furthermore, one can see from the graph that the greater the deviation from standard volume, the greater the volume variance.

Exhibit 5-6
Overhead
Variances

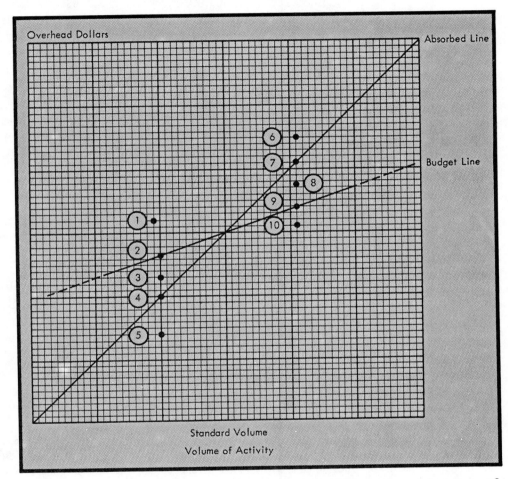

VOLUME OF ACTIVITY

The volume of activity used in this analysis can be measured in terms of either units completed or standard labor-hours, which express the standard labor content of units completed. If the department does only part of the work required to complete units, the volume of activity should reflect the partly completed units or the standard direct labor content of the partly completed work. As noted earlier, labor-hours are used more frequently than units because they are a measure that can be used throughout a production process that may involve many different kinds of units (pounds, feet, parts, components, etc.) and because labor-hours are often thought to be more closely related to overhead expenditures. If product design changes or if processing methods are altered, output units may remain unchanged, but the labor required could be quite different. Since much of overhead is related to people, accountants reason that a people-related measure should be used to predict the amount of overhead allowed. The labor content of what is produced is such a measure.

The measure of activity is usually stated as an output measure. Both units produced and standard labor content of units produced are measures of output or work accomplished. Inputs to a process, such as actual labor-hours or actual units put in process, are less frequently used as measures of activity. The main reason that output measures are used is accounting simplicity. A cost center or department is credited for what is actually sent on to the next department or to finished goods. Overhead is absorbed in inventory on this basis. If actual hours or input units are used as a measure of activity, there will have to be an additional overhead variance to reflect that the amount applied on the basis of actual inputs may not be the same as the amount absorbed by actual outputs. This third overhead variance is called the *overhead efficiency variance* and reflects the over- or under-absorption of overhead caused by a variation in labor efficiency from standard. There are very few situations in which this additional overhead variance produces useful information, and consequently it is seldom used.

INTERPRETING VARIANCES

When negative variances occur in a standard cost system, they do not necessarily mean that something is wrong. They simply compare an earlier estimate with what actually occurred. There is always the possibility that the estimate was wrong or unrealistic in the first place. However, the variance does mean that a plan was not fulfilled, and nonfulfillment usually causes concern. If standards are used in decisions on scheduling, pricing, or product design, it is certainly important to know as soon as possible whether it is the standard or the level of performance that needs to be changed.

Variances indicate that performance was not as planned. The breakdown of variances into the labor, material and overhead components of production costs and the further breakdown into price and quantity or spending and volume variances, helps to define the precise nature of the difference between planned and actual performance. However, the variances cannot indicate the reasons for the difference. Before management can take any corrective action, it must interpret the variances to find out why they occurred.

Variances usually come as no great surprise to an alert management. It is often obvious that material spoilage is high, or that there is excessive machine down-time. Direct observation or production counts will often indicate right away whether things are going properly. Two examples will illustrate the use of direct production reporting. The manager of a glass making plant called for a daily record showing pounds of good pieces formed. With this information he could tell quickly and accurately whether the previous day's production was up to standard. In another instance the manager of an electrical products plant received a weekly report showing the ratio of people in the direct and indirect labor categories. These managers received monthly reports showing material and labor variances and usually knew in advance approximately what they would show.

However, variance reports do often reveal trends or aggregate positions. Day-to-day or detailed observation may not show that certain areas are creeping toward seriously out-of-standard conditions, or that many little deviations are adding up to a large variance. Variance reports are a convenient way of summing up total performance and comparing it to the predetermined plan.

CONTROLLABILITY

Any action aimed at correcting variances must consider the problem of controllability. Material usage variances may be caused by inexperienced or careless operators. They may also be caused by poor purchasing that brought in poor quality material. Labor inefficiency may be either a production departmental problem, a scheduling problem, a product design problem, or a sales problem (such as selling too many small orders). Or labor inefficiency may result from a company strategy of rapid expansion that necessitated hiring and training inexperienced operators.

Separating overhead variances into volume and spending variances clarifies their controllability. A foreman can be expected to control overhead spending variances but not volume variances. Use of supplies and indirect labor may be controllable, and variation from the budget may indicate that his or her performance is not what it should be. Maintenance and repair, which may be considered variable and somewhat controllable by a foreman, may on occasion vary inversely with volume. The time when work is slack and machines are idle may be the opportunity for overhaul and preventative maintenance. Even volume variances may be affected by a departmental foreman if supervisory skill influences the department's ability to process a backlog of work.

Clearly, management's job is to look behind the variance figures to see what the causes are and to determine whether and how changes should be made. Developing an accounting system that produces variances is therefore only the beginning of management's job. Determining what action to take and acting effectively are where management really earns its pay.

SUMMARY

In this chapter we have reviewed the basic processes of standard costing systems. From a costing system covering one product and one cost center, we went on to more complex systems handling multiple cost centers and multiple products.

Standard costing systems require an investment of effort to establish standards for price, rate, and quantity, and they require continual up-dating for changes in price, methods, product design and processes. Their value lies in providing standard costs for planning, pricing, and reviewing operations. The use of standard product costs enables development of variances. For material there are usually price and usage variances; for labor there are usually rate and efficiency variances; for overhead there cannot be price and rate variances in the usual sense. The total variance can be separated into volume and spending variances, and occasionally a third variance, called the overhead efficiency variance is computed. Variances from standard, while they seldom give management the reasons for deviation from plan, do provide a convenient and continual monitoring system that shows to what extent operations are proceeding according to plan.

6

Variable Costing

Some years ago the manufacturing vice president of a company making timing devices was asked by a firm across town if he could make some parts for the other firm, which was having trouble meeting a government contract deadline. The vice president knew that things were a bit slack at the moment at his plant (as was the case also with several similar plants nearby) so he said that he thought he could and would have his controller work up a price. The part would need precision machining, one assembly step, and packing.

After asking the controller for a price, the vice president, who had been around for many years, took out his own little black book of costs and worked up his own estimate. When the controller came back with a cost, the vice president nearly exploded. "It's that bloody overhead in the screw machine room," he said, "I've always thought that 325 percent was too high. This time I'll fix you, though. I'm going to move one of those screw machines across the hall into the assembly department where overhead is only 75 percent and then we'll be able to make a decent bid on this job."

The controller was so shaken that he talked it over with the firm's president. Eventually the debate led to adoption of a *variable costing system*.

Variable costing,[1] often called the less accurate name, *direct costing*, has frequently been described and promoted as a wonderful new accounting system that provides management radically improved tools for decision making. When all the smoke has cleared, however, one can see that the system does not use any new concepts, nor is it particularly radical in design. Its main advantage is that it is a useful discipline in cost accumulation, which, if not previously practiced, provides new and helpful information for many kinds of decisions.

Basically, variable costing involves

1. Categorizing all manufacturing costs as either fixed or variable. The methods used are those described in the earlier discussions on relevant costs. The variable costs usually consist of material, direct labor, and those elements of manufacturing overhead that are considered variable.

2. Maintaining inventory at cost values that include only variable costs.

3. Accounting for non-variable or fixed manufacturing costs as period expenses. They are not added to inventory (and consequently are not part of cost of goods sold) but are charged off during the accounting period in which they are incurred.

4. Changing the internal financial reporting so that company, division, and product line income statements automatically show variable gross margins (sales minus variable costs), figures that are essentially the same as the contribution discussed earlier.

In short, variable costing takes fixed manufacturing overhead out of inventory and cost of goods sold, calling it a period expense. Only these fixed costs are treated differently. It may seem a small change, but its implications can be revolutionary.

VARIABLE COSTING COMPARED TO FULL COSTING

You may remember that full costing, whether a standard costing system or not, distributes all manufacturing costs to the product. Variable costing distributes only variable manufacturing costs to the product. Variable costing is usually described as providing "new" information because most companies come to the system by shifting from a traditional full costing system. Thus, comparing the two systems will highlight the choices they offer. (Later in this chapter, however, we will point out that the two systems are not really mutually exclusive.)

Cost information is valuable only in the context of its use by management. Hence, we will examine the usefulness of variable costing for the types of management decisions described in Chapter 1. We can then determine whether variable costing provides information that is more useful, accurate, or relevant than that provided by the traditional full costing system.

---

[1] The alternative and more common system is called *full costing* or *full absorption costing*.

EVALUATING PRODUCT PROFITABILITY

To see how variable costing can assist in evaluating product profitability, let us consider two income statements for a company with a broad line of products.

The company income statement in Figure 6-1 shows the same net profit under full costing and variable costing. Profits will be the same under both systems as long as inventory remains level. (What happens when inventory changes will be explained later.) Under full costing, fixed and variable manufacturing costs are not separated. Under variable costing, they are separated—$40,000 variable and $30,000 fixed—a separation that allows the company to calculate its variable gross margin.

**Figure 6-1
Company Income
Statements**

(Inventory Level Unchanged)	Full costing	Variable costing
Sales	$100,000	$100,000
Variable Cost of Goods Sold		40,000
Variable Gross Margin		60,000
Fixed Manufacturing Cost		30,000
Full Cost of Goods Sold	70,000	
Gross Margin	30,000	30,000
Administrative & Selling	20,000	20,000
Net Profit Before Taxes	$ 10,000	$ 10,000

Figure 6-2 shows how income statements for one of the company's product lines would look under each system. Since in variable costing fixed manufacturing costs are not distributed to the various products but are instead charged off in total as a period cost, there is no entry beyond the variable gross margin. Our comparative question, then, is whether the variable gross margin is more useful for evaluating product profitability than the total gross margin.

The variable gross margin is really a ready-made figure representing contribution to fixed costs. This gross margin as a percentage of sales (sometimes called the profit/volume ratio or P/V ratio) should remain constant under various levels of volume. With this ratio, one can quickly calculate how a change in volume will affect profit.

**Figure 6-2
Product G-2
Income Statements**

(Inventory level unchanged)	Full costing	Variable costing
Sales (10,000 units)	$20,000	$20,000
Variable Cost of Goods Sold ($1.00 per unit)		10,000
Variable Gross Margin		$10,000
Fixed Manufacturing Cost		Not Available
Full Cost of Goods Sold ($1.50 per unit)	15,000	
Gross Margin	$ 5,000	

For example, in Figure 6-2, Product G-2 has a P/V ratio of .5 (variable gross margin divided by sales). If sales are expected to increase $2,000, this P/V ratio shows that the expected increase in profit is $1,000 (.5 × 2,000 − 1,000). The gross margin of 25% of sales (after full costs) is not helpful, because gross margin cannot be expressed to vary directly with sales volume.

One can also use the breaken analytical framework to show the difference between the two systems. The graph shown in Figure 6-3 uses the total company figures shown earlier in Figure 6-1. The dotted line shows how total manufacturing costs will vary with volume, according to a full costing system. In other words, the dotted line shows the total costs that will be absorbed into inventory and charged to cost of goods sold. The other total cost line shows the effect of separating fixed and variable costs, as is done under variable costing. Note that the full cost line is always below the revenue line, suggesting that there will always be some gross margin whatever the volume. Variable costing advocates say that this implication is an inaccurate and misleading representation of the way costs actually behave. They point out that variable costing shows that when volume is below 50,000, revenue will be below total costs and a loss will be sustained.

Figure 6-3

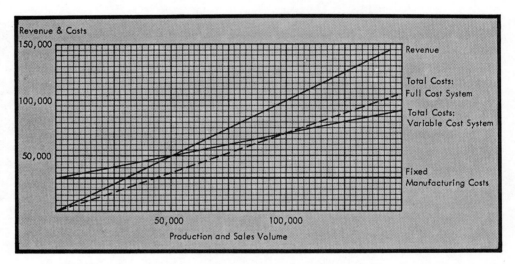

Classifying costs as fixed or variable certainly improves the evaluation of product profitability under varying volumes. It is dangerous, however, to ignore fixed costs entirely or to assume they will always remain fixed. Fixed costs have a way of staying the same for a while and then jumping up when an accumulation of capacity pressures forces a decision to expand or change a process. Theoretically every decision should have its own classification of costs but except for major decisions, the reclassification effort would not be worthwhile. Thus, the variable gross margin figure aids many management decisions but its accuracy should be accepted with caution.

Some companies develop two levels of variable gross margin to provide two types of contribution. The following table shows variable margin com-

	Product A	Product B
Sales........................	1,000	2,000
Variable Costs................	550	1,600
Variable Margin..............	450	400
Product Related Fixed Costs.....	300	50
Product Contribution..........	150	350

puted in the usual way. From this margin is subtracted product related fixed costs, which are those costs which, though fixed in the usual sense, are directly applicable to the product. Depreciation on machinery specially designed for the product and the product manager's salary are examples. While fixed for varying sales volumes, these costs could be avoided if the product were dropped. Thus, they are variable for the decision to keep or drop the product.

The two levels of contribution are useful for different decisions. The variable margin is useful for decisions on pricing, advertising and product design. The product contribution figure is not helpful for those decisions but does help in evaluating what kind of business to be in.

PRICING

It has been said that sales managers love variable costing while manufacturing managers distrust it. The reason for these preferences is that with only variable costs included, product costs will be lower, and the sales manager will have an easier argument for lower prices, which lead to more sales and happier salesmen. When the manufacturing vice president in the story at the beginning of this chapter wanted to cut his overhead by moving the screw machine into the assembly department, he was acting just like a sales manager.

Most manufacturing managers, on the other hand, focus on all those overhead costs that must be covered by sales revenue and fear that if margins are narrowed too much, overhead may never be covered.

Certainly enlightened management should have no difficulty overcoming this dilemma. One can have the best of both worlds, either by adding appropriate percentage margins onto variable costs or by using a full costing system that clearly separates fixed and variable costs so that marginal costs can be analyzed.

DETERMINING PROFIT VARIATIONS WHEN INVENTORY CHANGES

Variable costing introduces one bothersome difference in profits, which appears only when there is a change in inventory (work-in-process or finished goods).

If we start from the premise that manufacturing costs end up either in inventory or in cost of goods sold, or, under variable costing, become a period expense, then we can see how profits will be affected by inventory changes. The diagram shown below portrays the distribution of costs under both systems.

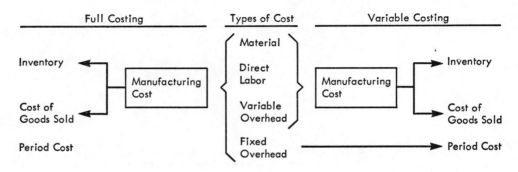

From this diagram, we can see that treatment of fixed overhead makes the difference. With variable costing, fixed overhead costs are always period costs and are expensed during the period. With full costing, they are expenses of the period only if the inventory of which they are a part is sold. If the inventory is not sold (inventory increases), some of the period's fixed costs will be capitalized, to be expensed later when the inventory is sold. (Also, one can see that if inventory decreases, some of last period's fixed costs are expenses this period.) The following examples will illustrate these discrepancies.

Suppose that finished inventory rises during the period from 1,000 to 1,500 units of Product G-2, described in Figure 6-2. The cost of inventory will look like this:

	Full costing		Variable costing	
	1,000 Units beginning	1,500 Units end	1,000 Units beginning	1,500 Units end
Variable Cost ($1.00/unit)			$1,000	$1,500
Full Cost ($1.50/unit)	$1,500	$2,250		
Increase		$750		$500

One can see that $750 has been added to inventory under the full costing system, but only $500 under variable costing. We know that costs not in inventory must be charged to the period. The $250 difference represents fixed costs that variable costing leaves out of inventory and charges to the period. Hence, variable costing will show $250 higher charges to the period and $250 lower profits; full costing, on the other hand, will show higher profits when inventory rises during the period. These differences are shown in Figures 6-4 and 6-5.

Figure 6-4 presents a period of G-2 sales and production in which production is constant at 10,000 units (as in Figure 6-2) but sales have decreased. Hence inventory rises and profits are $250 higher under full costing.

Figure 6-4 Inventory Rising: Production Constant, Sales Decrease

	Full costing	Variable costing
Sales (9,500 units at $2.00 ea.)	$19,000	$19,000
Cost of goods sold:		
Beginning inventory (1,000 units)	1,500	1,000
Variable cost of goods mfg. (10,000 units at $1.00)		10,000
Full cost of goods mfg. (10,000 units at $1.50)	15,000	
Less ending inventory (1,500 units)	(2,250)	(1,500)
Total cost of goods sold	$14,250	$ 9,500
Gross margin	$ 4,750	$ 9,500
Fixed manufacturing costs		5,000
Net before selling & administration	$ 4,750	$ 4,500

**Figure 6-5
Inventory Falling:
Production
Constant,
Sales Increase**

	Full costing	Variable costing
Sales (10,500 units at $2.00)	$21,000	$21,000
Cost of goods sold:		
Beginning inventory (1,500 units)	2,250	1,500
Variable cost of goods mfg. (10,000 units at $1.00)		10,000
Full cost of goods mfg. (10,000 units at $1.50)	15,000	
Less ending inventory (1,000 units)	(1,500)	(1,000)
Total cost of goods sold	$15,750	$10,500
Gross margin	$ 5,250	$10,500
Fixed manufacturing costs		5,000
Net before selling & administration	$ 5,250	$ 5,500

Figure 6-5 shows the effects of a reverse change in inventory. Sales have increased, inventory has decreased (production again constant), and profits are lower under full costing.

Figure 6-6 holds sales the same as in Figure 6-5 and increases production so that inventory increases and profits rise under full costing. It is sometimes said that when inventory rises under full costing, some fixed overhead is "sold to inventory" and hence avoids being a cost of the period. Of course, if inventory is reduced later on, the opposite effect will result. That high-cost inventory (full cost is higher than variable cost) will become cost of goods sold during the period and profits will be lower.

**Figure 6-6
Inventory Rising:
Production
Increased,
Sales Constant**

	Full costing	Variable costing
Sales (10,500 units at $2.00)	$21,000	$21,000
Cost of goods sold:		
Beginning inventory (1,000 units)	1,500	1,000
Variable cost of goods mfg. (11,000 units at $1.00)		11,000
Full cost of goods mfg. (11,000 units at $1.50)	16,500	
Less overabsorbed fixed costs*	(500)	
Less ending inventory (1,500 units)	(2,250)	(1,500)
Total cost of goods sold	$15,250	$10,500
Gross margin	$ 5,750	$10,500
Fixed manufacturing costs		5,000
Net before selling & administration	$ 5,750	$ 5,500

* Assuming actual fixed costs remain fixed at $5,000, production of 11,000 units would cause $5,500 to be absorbed (at $.50 per unit), hence the favorable overabsorption of $500.

One can summarize the effects as follows:

> When production exceeds sales, inventory rises, and profits are higher under full costing (lower under variable costing).

> When sales exceed production, inventory declines, and profits are lower under full costing (higher under variable costing).

One can also see that under variable costing, profits increase or decrease along with sales volume, and are unaffected by variations in production volume. (Compare Figure 6-6 with Figure 6-5.) This relationship exists because fixed production costs are charged to the period regardless of production or sales volumes. Under full costing, some of these fixed production costs may be left in or taken out of inventory, depending on the relative amounts of production and sales. Thus, variable costing advocates can say that since profits should reflect realized sales and not inventory changes, variable costing does a better job than full costing in presenting a reliable profit picture.

PLANNING INTER-DIVISIONAL SALES

When products are sold by one division to another, and perhaps after further work are sold again to a third division, an interesting phenomenon arises: fixed costs appear to be variable.

If Division A sells to Division B, the transfer price will normally cover all costs and perhaps provide a profit, too. From Division B's viewpoint, its purchase cost is variable; but from A's viewpoint, that transfer price is not all variable cost. It may include a large proportion of fixed costs.

The same relationships will exist when Division B sells to Division C. Then perhaps Division C sells to an outside customer. When Division C is doing its cost-volume-profit analysis, costs that are variable from its viewpoint will not be variable from the companywide viewpoint. (Division C may see 75% variable costs while in fact, for the company as a whole, they may be only 35% variable.) It is possible, then, that Division C might make a decision which is good for it but bad for the company as a whole.

Alleviating this problem is not easy. Two steps are necessary. One is to recognize the existence of the problem, and the second is to have available the fixed and variable split of all costs. This information would be available automatically if the company had a variable costing system.

VARIABLE COSTING AND EXTERNAL REPORTING

Variable costing is not generally accepted as a basis for external reporting. In 1957 the Committee on Accounting Concepts and Standards of the American Accounting Association stated that the reported cost of a manufactured product should not omit any element of manufacturing cost. Thus, inventory costs should include fixed manufacturing cost. Except for a few specialized exceptions, that report has been followed since 1957 in external, auditor-certified reporting.

A company using variable costing for internal purposes is therefore obliged to convert the variable cost of inventory to a full cost when preparing external financial statements. This conversion is commonly handled by adding an estimated amount of fixed cost based on an overall fixed cost-variable cost ratio.

SUMMARY
Variable costing is primarily used for internal management reporting. Its use obliges management to distinguish between fixed and variable costs and results in a variable gross margin (or contribution) measure of product profitability. This measure is more useful in short run decisions, that is, those decisions that affect only variable costs. Fixed manufacturing costs are considered to be a period cost and hence are unaffected by volume changes. In fact, some of those fixed costs tend to vary in the longer run. Thus, variable costing data on profitability should be used carefully.

A Matrix of
Cost System Choices

In previous chapters we have described a number of different ways costs can be collected, organized, and analyzed. In designing a system there are basically three pairs of choices which result in eight combinations. The three pairs of choices are as follows:

Actual cost or standard cost systems
Job cost or process costing systems
Full cost or variable costing systems

In order to emphasize the differences between cost systems, a three dimensional cost system matrix has proven useful in putting all major types in one framework. As shown in Figure 7-1, the matrix has eight compartments, four representing full cost systems and four representing the variable cost versions of the same four basic systems.

The text following Figure 7-1 gives a brief description of the four basic types of systems. It is worth noting that quadrant S II, containing the standard, process costing systems, has two parts, the second of which probably would not normally be described as a type of process costing system. This is a fairly common system for a company producing a variety of products, for which there are standard costs, but whose management has decided not to collect actual costs by product. Since actual costs are collected by time period, it is classified here as a process costing system. With this system, variances can be developed by department or process, but cannot be related to the individual product or lot. This highlights the fact that the distinctive feature of process costing systems is the method used to collect actual costs (by time period, not by product) rather than that costs are collected by process, or that the products produced are homogeneous.

Figure 7-1
Cost System
Matrix

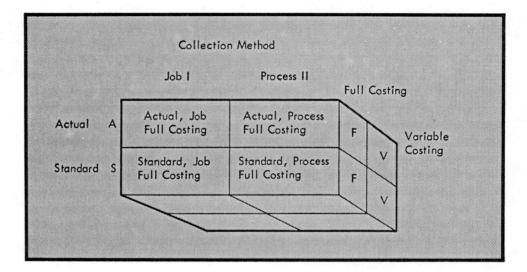

In order to clarify the trade-offs involved in choosing between systems, it is useful to consider what changes in information gathering and reporting would result from a shift from one quadrant to another. For example, shifting from a process to a job costing system would require measuring costs, or specifically, the costs of labor, material and overhead inputs, that are associated with a job, or some unit of output less than what is produced in the accounting period. Or considering a different choice, going from an actual job cost system to a standard job cost system would require establishing standard product costs, but would allow inventories to be kept at standard cost and facilitate the development of variances.

Any one of the basic systems can be either a full cost or variable cost system. This choice has been thoroughly discussed in the earlier chapter with particular attention to the advantages and disadvantages of each. The primary purpose of this matrix, therefore, is to focus on the differences among the four main classifications, any of which can be set up as either full cost or variable cost systems.

ACTUAL, JOB
FULL COSTING

Actual costs collected (may use standard labor rates or standard material prices) for each job, lot or order. Some sort of job sheet is often used. No standard quantities are used in cost system. A standard rate may be used to apply overhead.

Illustration: A job printer collects costs on each job by having the operators record times on job ticket accompanying the work. Each job is different. Job costs are obtained by multiplying operator times by a predetermined full cost rate and totalling cost of all operations.

ACTUAL PROCESS, FULL COSTING
Costs are collected for a time period and related to the units produced during the time period to get actual cost per unit. Work-in-process may be assumed not to vary or may be computed using equivalent units of production. For the latter, the extent of completion of work-in-process may be estimated to be constant (e.g., all units at 50%) or may be computed from direct observation.

Illustration: A paper company producing various widths and thicknesses of paper accumulates all direct and overhead costs of running the paper making machine and at month-end computes cost per pound produced.

STANDARD, JOB FULL COSTING
Standard quantities (labor hours and material amounts) are computed ahead of time, usually at the beginning of the year. Actual quantities are collected on job sheets (or time cards) and variances can be computed right away. Variances are linked to each item or lot produced.

Illustration: A ball bearing manufacturer has computed standard costs for each size and type of bearing. Actual times and quantities are noted on the job ticket accompanying each lot. For each lot produced, actual costs incurred in each operation can be compared with standard costs.

STANDARD PROCESS, FULL COSTING
Costs for a department or process are collected for a time period.

1. If units are to be considered as homogeneous, then the number of units produced times their standard cost is the output at standard cost. Comparison with actual inputs produces variances. Equivalent units of production may be used to value work-in-process.

Illustration: A bottling machine fills and caps bottles all month. The predetermined standard cost per bottle is compared at the end of the month with the average actual cost per bottle.

2.   If units are not homogeneous, then the number of each unit times its standard cost gives the standard cost of production of that unit. The total standard cost of all units is then compared to the total actual cost of inputs to produce variances. Equivalent production must be computed or assumed for each type of unit. Variances cannot be linked to a particular product.

Illustration: A food company assembles, cooks and freezes various kinds of TV dinners and pot pies. Each item has a predetermined standard cost of ingredients, labor and overhead. At the end of the month the total actual costs of ingredients, labor and overhead are compared with the standard cost of whatever was produced that month. For example, the total standard cost of chicken in all of the items containing chicken would be compared with the actual cost of chicken used.

VARIABLE COSTING SYSTEMS

The four variable costing systems are the same as the four just described except that only variable costs are considered. Fixed costs are not attached to products but are expensed directly in the period during which they are incurred.

part three

capital budgeting

INTRODUCTION   Capital expenditure analysis, often called capital budgeting, is performed in situations in which funds may be invested to realize increased profits or savings in the future. Such investments include constructing a manufacturing plant to produce and sell a new product or purchasing a new machine tool to save direct labor costs or to improve quality, which in turn leads to higher profits. The essential characteristic of these opportunities is that they involve some current investment, commitment, or outlay of funds to realize expected future benefits. The key question in analyzing capital expenditures is always, are the expected future benefits large enough, compared to the initial investment, to warrant the expenditure?

Difficulties arise with these decisions because a choice must often be made among competing alternatives. Frequently an organization will have only a limited amount of funds for such expenditures, and it wants to insure that the maximum benefit is derived from the investment. In other cases, ample funds may be available, but then the problem is to assure that they not be wasted in projects with little or no payoff.

The term *capital budgeting* stems from the fact that an organization with limited capital funds, specified goals and objectives, and several investment alternatives must carefully analyze and evaluate each alternative to select the "best" one. This selection or listing of recommended projects is called the *capital budget*. The process of judging a particular alternative prior to its inclusion in the capital budget is called *project evaluation*.

Evaluating Capital Expenditures

IMPORTANCE OF CAPITAL EXPENDITURES

Capital budgeting decisions are among the most important decisions an organization makes because they tie the company to long-term commitments in equipment, plants, products, special programs, and the like. In contrast, many day-to-day operating decisions can be reversed if future events change. For example, employment levels may be adjusted through terminations, attrition, or retirement; prices can be changed; new suppliers sought or old ones terminated. But plants are not so easily closed, nor special machines and equipment sold. Thus, the results of capital budgeting quickly become permanent. Furthermore, capital expenditures typically involve relatively large sums; consequently, such decisions are important for their magnitude as well as their permanence. Capital budgets reflect the long-range plans of an organization and are a means of implementing those plans.

FINANCIAL MEASUREMENT

The focus of this chapter is capital budgeting and project evaluation with respect to financial criteria. Financial considerations are normally the major if not the sole basis upon which investment decisions are made. The reasons are obvious. Businesses invest funds to return a profit to stockholders. They may increase this pool of available funds by borrowing or by other means, but only if they are able to invest this additional amount at a profit. Governments and foundations operate with only limited resources which must also be invested wisely.

While financial criteria are very important, it should be noted that not all investment decisions are made for economic reasons. Safety equipment is purchased to cut accidents and save lives. Pollution control devices are installed to prevent contamination of air or water. Governments, foundations, and even businesses make investments for social rather than economic reasons. In an emergency a company may buy a new generator or tractor or computer in order to get a factory or office back into operation, no matter what the cost. Sometimes a decision is made on personal grounds, as when the owner-manager of a company decides to build a new office in a particular city because that's where he wishes to live. Even in these cases, however, the financial implications are often assessed. In many other situations financial considerations are but one of a number of criteria. This chapter's primary concern, however, will be the financial considerations in capital budgeting decisions.

BASIC ELEMENTS OF CAPITAL BUDGETING

The capital budgeting process can be viewed as consisting of six parts:

1.   Collecting ideas.

2.   Developing alternatives.

3.   Estimating results.

4.   Evaluating alternatives.

5.   Considering risk.

6.   Preparing the capital budget.

Each of these elements is discussed below.

Collecting Ideas

In any large organization ideas for change requiring capital expenditures are continually arising at all levels and for a variety of reasons: to cut costs, increase capacity, develop new products, improve quality, etc. New ideas are vital to any successful organization, and some procedure or mechanism must be established to collect and analyze them. Some organizations are better at this than others. The key to success at this first step is the ability to encourage all types of new ideas and thus to nurture this creative process while at the same time quickly but carefully screening the ideas to select only the most promising for detailed, thorough analysis. This balance is a very delicate one, for a harsh screening process may eliminate good ideas from further consideration while a weak one allows expensive and scarce analysis effort to be devoted to too many worthless ideas. Once a "good idea" has been identified, the next step is to determine how best to exploit it. Often a number of alternatives present themselves.

Developing Alternatives

Capital budgeting decisions always involve a selection among alternatives. Even if at first glance there appears to be only one option (for example, the opportunity to invest in a new labor saving machine or to build a plant to produce a new product), further analysis usually uncovers additional alternatives—if only that of the status quo, that is, to do nothing. Indeed, many decisions involve comparisons against the status quo. However, if only one course of action is in fact possible, then one does not have a problem for no decision need be made.

Discovering new ideas and developing alternative courses of action are undoubtedly the most important aspects of the capital budgeting process. It is obvious that no matter how much attention is paid to estimating cash flow, calculating paybacks, and making other evaluations, *if the best alternatives are not even considered, then only a poor decision can result.* Identifying additional alternatives can be quite difficult. For example, a company might come up with the idea of investing in a small computer to automate a manual payroll operation. There are apparently two alternatives: to invest in the small computer or to continue the present operation. But further study might uncover many more alternatives, including

1. Improved manual operation.

2. Partial automation via business machines.

3. Use of a computer service bureau.

4. Purchase of a large computer capable of automating other functions besides payroll, such as inventory control and production scheduling.

In fact, the best alternative might be to abandon the payroll process altogether and arrange for a bank to do payroll accounting and to make direct deposits to employees' accounts. Obviously, selecting the best alternative requires thorough analysis of each; yet without the full list of alternatives, the best might be overlooked. Unfortunately, many capital budgeting decisions are doomed from the start because the best choice is never considered.

Estimating Results

An essential step in project evaluation is estimating the results of each alternative: its future profits or savings and its future costs. Even determining the total cost of the initial investment may require an estimate; for example, the exact price of a new piece of machinery can be determined from the seller, but the costs of freight, installation, wiring, and perhaps the resale value of the old equipment may require estimates. In preparing these estimates one normally attempts to establish the "most likely" figure for profit or savings. Sometimes a separate "conservative" or "optimistic" schedule of estimates is prepared, and the results are then compared to those of the "most likely" estimate. In every case, however, it is important to be sure that the estimates are prepared carefully. A useful set of guidelines to follow are

1. *Be honest.* Estimating future savings or costs is not the time to bring personal preferences into the analysis.

2. *Be consistent.* Don't mix conservative estimates with the most likely or the optimistic.

3. *Use rounded figures.* Estimates of future events cannot normally be made precisely. Figures to six decimal points or to the penny suggest a degree of precision that may be unwarranted. Rounded figures are also easier to manipulate mathematically.

4. *Collect data wisely.* Better data may enable a better decision; sometimes an organization will spend several thousand dollars and many months of effort just to collect data for a decision. This is another trade-off or balancing situation—collecting more data usually costs more money and takes time, thus delaying the decision; but better data may yield a better solution. The decision as to when to stop collecting data and make a decision based upon the evidence at hand is always difficult yet very important.

5. *Don't estimate beyond a reasonable horizon.* Estimates should be made no further into the future than can be reasonably anticipated. For example, when a new machine tool is considered, estimates of savings beyond ten years are normally not made. The entire factory might be sold or scrapped by that time.

The last point is particularly important. Special attention should be given to what is called the "economic life" of a project or alternative. Very few capital budgeting alternatives have unlimited lives. Often the expected life of a machine or product can be estimated and used as the economic life. Sometimes the decision is arbitrary: "We can't look beyond 60 months on this deal; the chances of keeping the product going past that time are just too low." Whatever time span is selected, the important thing is to *be sure that the same span is used to evaluate each alternative.* In the payroll example mentioned above, the results of each alternative must be estimated for the same time period. Otherwise, the alternatives are not really comparable. More will be said about this later.

In capital budgeting decisions, estimates of the total investment and its savings, costs, and profits are usually made in terms of cash flow rather than accounting income or savings. In many situations there is little difference between income statements results and cash flow. Cash flow from sales closely follows accounting sales (on the income statement). Savings in labor, materials, supplies, etc., are frequently actual cash flow savings.

However, income statement and cash flow frequently differ regarding depreciation and book values. Depreciation is an expense item on the income statement recognizing a portion of the cost of an asset over time. But although it tends to reduce net income, depreciation is not a cash expense—cash was only spent at the time that the asset was originally purchased. That cash outlay made sometime in the past is a sunk cost and cannot be affected by any decision made now.[1]

The book value of a machine scrapped when a new machine is purchased represents the unallocated amount of the original purchase price. But book values seldom represent market values if the asset is sold or scrapped. Since we are interested in cash flows that result from a proposed decision, it is the scrap value or resale value that is relevant, not the book value, unless they happen to be the same. However, the book value will affect taxes, and tax payments are cash flows. Generally, the write-off of book value will come either all at once if the machine is scrapped or over time as a depreciation charge. Thus, the difference is primarily one of timing. There will be more discussion of depreciation and book value later in the section of this chapter on dealing with taxes.

In comparing alternatives, one usually needs to specify only their differing results. For example, if we are considering the purchase of a semi-automatic or an automatic packaging machine to replace the existing manual operation, all we will be concerned with are the changes in future cash flows under each alternative. We do not need to concern ourselves with all future costs—just with those that will be affected by the investment in either machine. Also, we do not need to estimate the total plant costs five years from now—only the changes in costs. This type of estimation is usually termed a *differential analysis*.

Evaluating Alternatives

Several techniques exist for evaluating capital budgeting alternatives. Each method has certain advantages as well as disadvantages, and it is essential that the decision maker be aware of each while using a particular technique. The four techniques to be discussed here are the ones most often used in business today:

1. Payback.

2. Unadjusted rate of return.

3. Net present value.

4. Internal rate of return.

I. PAYBACK

The purpose of the payback method is to determine *when* the funds invested in a particular project will be recovered through profits or savings. The result is expressed as a period of time, such as three months or 6 1/2 years. The payback technique addresses the question: If we spend $10,000 on a labor-saving machine, *how long will it take us to recover our investment through savings*? If we save $2,000 per year, the payback is *five years*. If $5,000 per year, the payback is *two years*.

---

[1] For a more detailed discussion of sunk costs, see Chapter 3.

When payback is calculated, savings or inflows are normally based on cash flows rather than on accounting or book profits. Also cash savings are calculated net of applicable income taxes. When the savings are uniform (the same each time period), payback can be calculated as

$$\text{Payback} = \frac{\text{Investment}}{\text{Annual Cash Savings}}$$

For example, suppose a $10,000 machine saves $4,000 per year in labor costs and will be used for 5 years, the depreciation life of the machine. What is the payback if the company expects its income taxes to be 50%? To figure the payback, we first need to determine the yearly cash flow. It is $3,000, calculated as follows:

$4,000	Annual Book Savings
(2,000)	Less Depreciation Expense
2,000	Taxable Savings
1,000	Income Taxes (50%)
1,000	After Tax Savings
2,000	Add Back Depreciation
$3,000	After Tax Cash Savings

In words, what we've done here is to recognize that while we expect $4,000 in yearly labor savings, we must consider depreciation expense and income taxes as well. Depreciation is $10,000/5 or $2,000 per year. Thus, taxable savings are only $2,000; after tax savings, just $1,000. However, depreciation is not a cash expense, so it must be added back to get after tax cash savings of $3,000. (Calculating cash flows is described more fully in the section on dealing with taxes.) Using the formula, we find the payback to be 3.33 years:

$$\text{Payback} = \frac{\text{Investment}}{\text{Annual Cash Savings}} = \frac{10,000}{3,000} = 3.33 \text{ years.}$$

When the return is not the same each year, payback can only be determined by a process of counting or accumulation. For example, if our $10,000 machine is expected to yield the cash savings shown in Column 1 of the table below, the savings accumulate as in Column 2.

Table 8-1

Year	(1) Cash savings	(2) Accumulated savings
1	$1,000	$ 1,000
2	1,000	2,000
3	3,000	5,000
4	3,000	8,000
5	4,000	12,000
6	4,000	16,000
7	4,000	20,000

Payback is that point at which the investment is just recovered—in this case, 4 1/2 years. At the beginning of year *4* we would have recovered $8,000, and, assuming an equal cash flow throughout the year, we would receive the remaining $2,000 by mid-year of the fifth year.

Payback analysis has several advantages. The method is simple and the calculations are straightforward. More important, the concept of payback, the end result, is readily understood. Payback is also used by many people to deal with risk. One might ask, "How long must we count on getting these savings before we break even?" However, as we shall show later, it is a very crude and often inaccurate technique for this purpose.

Unfortunately, the payback approach has several disadvantages, the most serious of which is that it ignores any revenue or savings beyond the payback period. The following two investments both have the same payback yet Alternative B earns cash flow for several years beyond that of A and its total cash flow is much higher.

Alternatives A and B

Alternative A	Alternative B
Investment: $15,000	Investment: $15,000

Alternative A			Alternative B		
Cash Flow:	*Year*	*Amount*	Cash Flow:	*Year*	*Amount*
	1	$5,000		1	$6,000
	2	5,000		2	5,000
	3	5,000		3	4,000
				4	3,000
				5	2,000

Alternative A	Alternative B
Payback = 3 years	Payback = 3 years

From this example the reader will note that payback measures return *of* investment (how long must we wait to get back what we put in?), not of return *on* investment (how much do we get back compared to what we put in?). The three other techniques we will introduce all measure return *on* investment.

II. UNADJUSTED RATE OF RETURN

Investors often calculate the return on investment (ROI) of a company by dividing the profit for the year by the company's investment in land, buildings, and equipment, etc. When this approach is used to evaluate capital budgeting alternatives, it is called the unadjusted rate of return or the accountant's method. The unadjusted rate of return is calculated by dividing the annual average savings, minus depreciation, by the average investment outstanding. The savings or profit figures are accounting or book income rather than cash flow. Average investment is often taken to be one-half of the purchase costs.

$$\text{Unadjusted Rate of Return} = \frac{\text{Average Annual Saving}}{\text{Average Investment}}$$

For example, if a $10,000 investment is expected to yield $4,000 each year for five years, the unadjusted rate of return is 40%.

$$\text{Return} = \frac{4,000 - 2,000}{(10,000/2)} = 40\%$$

(The $2,000 is the depreciation.)

Savings are generally taken before taxes, although in some companies the calculation is done on an after-tax basis. Gross investment (purchase costs not halved), is sometimes used rather than average investment; the investment figure chosen makes little difference in comparing alternatives as long as a company uses the same approach to evaluate each alternative.

Unadjusted rate of return is also simple to compute, easy to understand, and widely used. Its greatest weakness is that it operates under the assumption that money received or spent today is worth the same as money received or spent in the future. For example, look at the following alternatives.

Alternatives C and D

Alternative C

Investment: $10,000

Year	Savings
1	$2,000
2	3,000
3	4,000
4	5,000
5	6,000

Average Annual Savings:

$20,000/5 or $4,000

Unadjusted Rate of Return:

$$\frac{4,000 - 2,000}{5,000}$$

or 40%

Alternative D

Investment: $10,000

Year	Savings
1	$6,000
2	5,000
3	4,000
4	3,000
5	2,000

$20,000/5 or $4,000

$$\frac{4,000 - 2,000}{5,000}$$

or 40%

Each alternative has an unadjusted rate of return of 40%, but clearly D is superior to C, for we receive our money sooner and we can then presumably invest it somewhere else. The technique has ignored the time value of money. In the above problem the advantages of receiving the money earlier are readily apparent by visual inspection; no one would be foolish enough to think the two alternatives were equal. But suppose that another alternative were found.

Alternative E

Investment: $10,000

Year	Savings
1	$6,000
2	6,000
3	6,000
4	500
5	500

Average Annual Savings: $19,000/5 = $3,800

Unadjusted Rate of Return: $\frac{\$3,800 - 2,000}{\$5,000} = 36\%$

Here the unadjusted rate of return is less than 40%. Using the unadjusted rate of return method, we would discard Alternative E from further study, but quick inspection shows that this alternative earns savings of $18,000 during the first three years while D yields $15,000 and C only $9,000. Isn't it possible that if it's worth enough to us to have our money sooner rather than later, Alternative E would be preferable to D or C? This question leads us to consider *present value* and its use in the time adjusted rate of return method.

Present Value

The time value of money. As we've already noted, the value of money to us changes over time. If we are to be paid $1,000, we'd prefer to have it today rather than next year, since if we had it today we could invest it and have more than $1,000 by this time next year. Another reason for preferring to get our money sooner rather than later is that during periods of inflation the "real" or economic value of money declines. Thus, we'd prefer our payment in current dollars than future, lower-valued dollars. The methods necessary to deal properly with anticipated inflation are discussed in Chapter 10 of this book. For the remainder of this chapter we shall reflect just the cost or value of money apart from the effects of inflation.

If we were to invest $1,000 in a bank paying 5% interest, by next year we'd have $1,050. In fact, we'd only have to invest $952 today to have $1,000 next year. [Five percent interest on $952 would give us $48 (.05 x 952). This together with the return of our $952 totals $1,000.] This leads us to a very important conclusion: receiving $1,000 one year from now is not "worth" $1,000 to us now, it's only "worth" $952. Another way of viewing this is that at 5% we're indifferent as to a $952 payment now or $1,000 in one year. This $952 amount is called the *present value* of the $1,000 payment to be received in one year and this approach is called *discounting*.

Also note that present value works whether we're being *paid* or *paying someone*. At 5% we're indifferent as to *paying* $952 now or $1,000 a year from now. We're also indifferent as to *receiving* $952 now or $1,000 one year from now.

If we had other opportunities to invest that would yield more than 5%, the $1,000 future payment would be worth even less than $952. Thus, present value is dependent upon some interest rate—in our example 5%. It is also clear that if the $1,000 were to be received 10 years from today, it would be "worth" even less than $952. Thus, present value is dependent upon some *time period* as well. Therefore, to be precise, we say:

The present value at 5% of $1,000 received one year from now is $952.

Tables exist which provide a present value factor for a large combination of interest rates and periods of time.[2] Table I in the Appendix of this chapter

---

[2] The mathematics for determining present value are quite simple:

$$\text{Present Value} = \frac{\text{Future Payment}}{(1 + i)^n}$$

when (i) is the rate of interest and (n) is the number of years until the time of payment. In our sample problem (i) was .05 (5%) and (n) was 1 (one year) so that:

$$\text{Present Value} = \frac{\$1,000}{(1.05)^1} = \$952.$$

For most problems the decision maker has access to a table of present value factors or a computer program for these calculations.

gives present value factors for interest rates from 2%-30% and from 1-40 years. To use this table one must first locate the present value factor corresponding to the interest rate and time period in question. The factor from the table is then multiplied by the amount to be received to yield the present value.

For example, suppose a company is to receive $5,000 at the end of 12 years and money, to them, is worth 8%. What is the present value of that future payment?

Looking at Table I we find the present value factor for 12 years at 8% to be .40. Multiplying this times the $5,000 yields a present value of $2,000.

In another case, suppose that we are to receive three equal payments of $5,000; the first at the end of year 1, the second at the end of year 2, and the last at the end of year 3. What is the present value of these payments at 8%? Table 8-2 shows this calculation using Table I.

Table 8-2

(1)	(2)	(3)	(4)
			(Column 2 × 3)
		Table I	
End of year	*Cash flow*	*present value factor*	*present value*
1	$5,000	.93	$ 4,650
2	5,000	.86	4,300
3	5,000	.79	3,950
		Total	$12,900

The present value at 8% of $5,000 each year for three years is $12,900.

Since we frequently find capital budgeting problems involving *equal annual cash flows* (Table 8-2), tables exist to make this calculation directly. Such present value factors are shown in Table III of Appendix. Thus, from Table III the present value factor for three equal yearly payments at 8% is 2.58; and 2.58 times $5,000 is $12,900.[3] Table III just saves a good deal of time and calculation whenever the cash flows are equal.

In each of the above examples, the cash flow occurred as a single payment or payments *at the end of the year*. What about situations where the cash flows occur more or less evenly throughout the year as would normally happen with profits from a new product or savings from a new machine? Approximate present value factors for continuous cash flows provided in Table II (for a mid-year payment during any one year) and the Table IV (for equal annual cash flows occurring during the year). Since it *does* make a difference, the decision maker must be careful to determine the actual timing of the expected cash flows for each problem and then use the appropriate table.

III. Net Present Value

How is present value used as a technique to evaluate capital budgeting alternatives? The steps are as follows:

---

[3] The reader will note that 2.58 is simply the sum of three present value factors: .93, .86, and .79. Indeed, that is how Table III was derived.

1. First, determine the *required investment rate*, or "hurdle rate," which represents the organization's cost of funds or the earnings rate that a new investment must exceed to be approved. For some companies this rate is set at the average cost of money (both from debt and from equity) for the firm. In other organizations the hurdle rate is set higher to eliminate all but the most profitable investment alternatives. Organizations often separate capital expenditures into one of several categories according to the riskiness of the project, establishing different hurdle rates for each category. Ordinarily, the same hurdle rate is used for all capital budgeting decisions within the same risk category, and this rate remains the same over a long period of time. Determining this investment rate is a very important step in the net present value method, but any further discussion of it is beyond the scope of this chapter.

2. *Estimate* the total *cash investment* for each alternative. If the investment is made at the beginning of a project, no discounting is necessary because cash is paid immediately. This investment is usually referred to as a cash flow in time period 0 (hence a discount or present value factor of 1).

3. *Estimate* the resulting *cash savings* in the future, period by period.

4. *Discount* or determine the present value of these future cash flows using present value factors for each year at the required investment rate.

5. Add the discounted figures together. The total is the *sum of the discounted cash flows*.

6. Subtract the original investment from the sum of the discounted cash flows. The result is net present value. If net present value is positive, this alternative exceeds the investment rate, or hurdle rate. If negative, the alternative fails to meet the required return.

For example, using Alternatives C and D shown earlier and assuming that 8% is the hurdle rate, or minimum acceptable rate of return, we perform the following calculations.

Alternative C

(1)	(2)	(3)	(4)	(5)
	Unadjusted cash flow	*Present value factor*	*Discounted cash flow (Col. (2)*	
Time period	*(+savings) (−investment)*	*8% (from Table I)*	*× Col. (3))*	*Adjusted cash flow*
0	−$10,000	1.0		−$10,000
1	+ 2,000	.93	$ 1,860	
2	3,000	.86	2,580	
3	4,000	.79	3,160	
4	5,000	.73	3,650	
5	6,000	.68	4,080	
Sum of the discounted cash flows			$15,330	+$15,330
Net present value				$ 5,330

Alternative D

(1) Time period	(2) Unadjusted cash flow (+savings) (−investment)	(3) Present value factor 8% (from Table I)	(4) Discounted cash flow (col. (2) × col. (3))	(5) Adjusted cash flow
0	−$10,000	1.0		−$10,000
1	6,000	.93	$ 5,580	
2	5,000	.86	4,300	
3	4,000	.79	3,160	
4	3,000	.73	2,190	
5	2,000	.68	1,360	
Sum of the discounted cash flows			$16,590	+$16,590
Net present value				$ 6,590

From these examples, we can see that since both alternatives have a positive net present value, both projects exceed the 8% investment rate requirement. We also see that at the 8% rate Alternative D has a higher net present value. Other things being equal and if the alternatives are mutually exclusive (i.e., only one of the alternatives can be selected), D would be preferred.

DEALING WITH TAXES

Most of the discussions to date have dealt with current investments and future cash flows as if income taxes were not an issue in the decision. Indeed, many organizations that face capital budgeting decisions do not pay income taxes: schools, municipal hospitals, governmental agencies, foundations, etc. However, most business organizations do pay both federal and state income taxes; and since taxes do affect investment decisions, they must be considered.

Taxes enter the evaluation of capital budgeting decisions in two ways: (1) some or all of the savings may be subject to tax, and (2) some or all of the initial investment may be depreciated or amortized in the future, serving to reduce taxable earnings at that time. The latter consideration often causes confusion because while depreciation reduces taxable income and thus reduces cash *outflow* (cash that otherwise would have gone to pay taxes), depreciation itself is not a cash expense. For example, assume that the investment in Alternative E had an expected life of five years for tax purposes. Note that this time span also corresponds to the length of expected savings and is the economic life. Suppose also that a straight-line method of depreciation is to be used. We then make the following calculations on the next page.

Note that during the first three years the $6,000 before-tax savings amounts to $4,000 savings after tax. Again, this discrepancy results from two factors:

Alternative E

Time period	(1)	(2) Unadjusted cash flow (+savings) (−investment)	(3) Present value factor 8% (from Table I)	(4) Discounted cash flow (col. (2) × col. (3))	(5) Time adjusted cash flow
0		−$10,000	1.0		−$10,000
1		+4,000*	.93	$ 3,720	
2		4,000*	.86	3,440	
3		4,000*	.79	3,160	
4		1,250†	.73	912	
5		1,250†	.68	850	
				$12,082	+$12,082

Net present value $ 2,082

Derivation of unadjusted cash flow, column 2 above:

Description	* Years 1–3	† Years 4–5	
Total savings	$6,000	$ 500	
Depreciation	−2,000	−2,000	
Taxable savings	$4,000	($1,500)	(Loss)
Taxes	2,000	(750)	(Taxes avoided)
Therefore:			
Total savings	$6,000	$ 500	
Less taxes	2,000	(750)	(Taxes avoided)
Unadjusted cash flow	$4,000	$1,250	

1.   Taxes on $6,000 savings at 50% are $3,000, leaving $3,000 after-tax cash flow.

2.   But, depreciation of $2,000/year "saves" $1,000 in taxes, leaving $4,000 ($3,000 + $1,000) as the *total after-tax cash flow*.

An alternative form of calculation, shown in Table 8-3 uses data from Alternative D. Again, a tax life of 5 years and income tax rate of 50% is assumed. The arrangement of this table is designed to prevent the kinds of errors in analysis that can easily occur when the tax rate is not 50%. These matters can become very tricky; at a 40% tax rate, every $1 of savings before tax leaves 60¢ after tax, but every $1 of depreciation only saves 40¢ in taxes.

Table 8-3
Evaluation of Alternative D

Description	(1) Time period	(2) Savings	(3) Depreciation	(4) Taxable savings	(5) (4) × Tax rate Tax	(6) (2) − (5) After tax cash flow	(7) Table I 8% present value factor	(8) (6) × (7) Discounted cash flow	Totals
Investment	0					−10,000	1.0		−10,000
	1	+6,000	2,000	4,000	2,000	+4,000	.93	+3,720	
	2	5,000	2,000	3,000	1,500	3,500	.86	3,010	
	3	4,000	2,000	2,000	1,000	3,000	.79	2,370	
	4	3,000	2,000	1,000	500	2,500	.73	1,825	
	5	2,000	2,000	−0−	−0−	2,000	.68	1,360	12,285
						Net present value			2,285

Replacement or Scrapping. When one asset is replaced by another, the old asset is often sold for either a profit or a loss with respect to taxes. Scrapping an old asset also may yield tax advantages Disposition of the old asset can create three basic situations:

1. Scrapping an old asset (disposing of an old asset and receiving nothing for it).

2. Loss on sale of old asset (selling an old asset, but at some price less than book value).

3. Gain on sale of old asset (selling an old asset at some price greater than book value).

We will illustrate each situation separately.

1. *Scrapping an Asset*

Old Asset:	Original Cost — $15,000 Accumulated Depreciation — $10,000 Scrap Value — $0 Remaining Life — 5 years
New Asset:	Cost — $20,000 Expected Life — 5 years Expected salvage at end of 5 years — $0
Savings on New Asset:	$6,000/year for 5 years
Required Investment Rate:	12%

Table 8-4 shows that the net present value at 12% is negative $355. Hence this investment does not quite meet the required investment rate of 12%.

Table 8-4
Scrapping an Asset

Description	Time period (1)	Savings (2)	Depreciation (3)	Taxable savings (4)	(4) × Tax rate Tax (5)	(2) − (5) After tax cash flow (6)	Table IV 12% present value factor (7)	(6) × (7) Discounted cash flow (8)
New investment	0					−20,000	1.0	−20,000
Tax savings on scrappage	0			(5,000)*	(2,500)	+2,500	1.0	+2,500
Future depreciation lost	1–5		(1,000)	(1,000)†	500	−500	3.81	−1,905
Savings	1–5	6,000	4,000	2,000	1,000	+5,000	3.81	+19,050
					Net Present Value			−355

* $15,000 Original cost
  10,000 Accumulated depreciation
$ 5,000 Book value
Thus, $5,000 before tax loss on scrappage yields $2,500 tax savings
† Tax savings on future depreciation given up.

There is an important point to observe from this example. When an asset is scrapped but has a remaining book value (accumulated depreciation is less than the original cost), a loss equal to the book value may be reported for tax purposes—in this case, $5,000. If the tax rate is 50%, this reporting will save $2,500 in cash flow that would otherwise have been paid in taxes. But had we continued to use the asset, we would have eventually been able to depreciate it to zero and thus realize the full $5,000 in depreciation (and hence save $2,500 in taxes). By scrapping the asset and taking this tax loss now, we forego taking depreciation and the resulting tax savings in the future ($500/year for 5 years or $2,500). Hence we save $2,500 in taxes whatever we decide to do, but there is an advantage to immediate scrapping because of the time value of money. From the above figures, we find that immediate scrapping saves $2,500 in taxes now, but we give up $500/year for 5 years, a sum that is "worth" only $1,905 at 12% now. (The present value of $500/year for 5 years at a 12% discount rate is $1,905.)

Another way of explaining this so-called depreciation tax savings foregone is to consider a situation in which a new machine is to be bought and there still is a question of whether the older machine is to be kept or scrapped.

Table 8-5

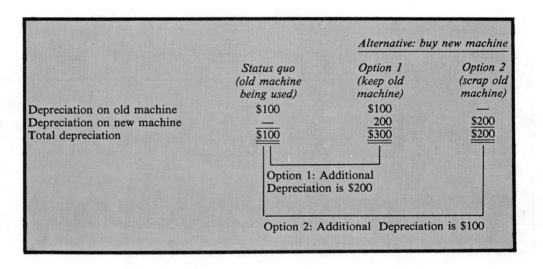

Suppose for purposes of this illustration that the old machine's depreciation is $100 while the new machine's depreciation will be $200. Clearly, if the old machine is kept when the new one is bought, then the total depreciation will $300 or *an increase* of $200. But if the old asset is replaced by the new one and scrapped, then the *additional depreciation* is only $100 (depreciation on the new asset is $200 but depreciation foregone on the scrapped machine is $100). The depreciation on the old machine is available as a tax shield whether a new machine is bought or not. But if the old machine is scrapped (and a tax loss taken at that time), then that machine's tax shield in the future is lost.

2. Loss on Sale of Asset

Old Asset:	Original Cost — $20,000 Accumulated Depreciation — $10,000 Sales Value — $5,000 Remaining Life — 5 years
New Asset:	Cost — $20,000 Expected Life — 5 years Expected salvage value at end of 5 years — $0
Savings on New Asset:	$6,000/year for 5 years
Required Investment Rate:	10%

Here we see that sale of the old asset yields an immediate $5,000 in cash flow plus a $5,000 book loss (old book value was $20,000 − $10,000 or $10,000). The $5,000 loss saves $2,500 in taxes so that the cash flow effect of the sale is $7,500 ($5,000 + $2,500). Had we not sold the asset, we would continue depreciating it at $2,000 per year, thus saving $1,000/year in tax. The depreciation tax savings given up is thus $1,000 per year for five years, which discounted at 10% is "worth" $3,980.

Table 8-6 shows that the net present value at 10% is positive $3,420. Hence this investment does meet the required investment rate of 10%.

Table 8-6
Loss on Sale of Asset

	(1)	(2)	(3)	(4)	(5)	(6)	(7)	(8)
Description	Time period	Savings	Depreciation	Taxable savings	(4) × Tax rate Tax	(2)—(5) After tax cash flow	Table IV 10% present value factor	(6) × (7) Discounted cash flow
Investment	0					−20,000	1.0	−20,000
Sale of old asset*	0					+5,000	1.0	+5,000
Tax savings on loss†	0			(5,000)	(2,500)	+2,500	1.0	+2,500
Future depreciation lost‡	1–5		(2,000)	(2,000)	(1,000)	−1,000	3.98	−3,980
Savings	1–5	6,000	4,000	2,000	1,000	+5,000	3.98	+19,900
					Net Present Value			+3,420

* Sales value of old asset
† Tax savings on loss on sale of old asset
‡ Tax savings on future depreciation given up

3.   *Gain on Sale of Asset*

Old Asset:	Original Cost — $20,000 Accumulated Depreciation — $10,000 Current Sales Value — $15,000 Remaining Life — 5 years
New Asset:	Cost — $20,000 Expected Life — 5 years Expected salvage value at end of 5 years — $0
Savings:	$6,000/year for 5 years
Required Investment Rate:	10%

Table 8-7 shows that the net present value at 10% is positive $8,420. Hence this investment surpasses the required investment rate of 10% by a wide margin.

Table 8-7
Gain on Sale of Asset

Description	(1) Time period	(2) Savings	(3) Depreciation	(4) Taxable savings	(5) (4) × Tax rate Tax	(6) (2)—(5) After tax cash flow	(7) Table IV 10% present value factor	(8) (6) × (7) Discounted cash flow
Investment	0					−20,000	1.0	−20,000
Sale of old asset*	0					+15,000	1.0	+15,000
Tax on gain†	0			5,000	2,500	−2,500	1.0	−2,500
Future depreciation lost‡	1–5		(2,000)	(2,000)	(1,000)	−1,000	3.98	−3,980
Savings	1–5	6,000	4,000	2,000	1,000	+5,000	3.98	+19,900
					Net present value			+8,420

* Sales value of old asset
† Taxes on gain on sale of old asset
‡ Tax savings lost on future depreciation given up

Advantages/Disadvantages of Net Present Value Method. The net present value method represents a significant improvement over the unadjusted rate of return approach in that it recognizes the time value of money and explicitly incorporates it into the calculations. However, it has several disadvantages:

1.   The calculations are more difficult.

2.   The meaning and importance of the time value of money must be thoroughly understood by the decision maker.

3.   The required investment rate must be known.

4.   The answers are difficult to interpret.

This last item is perhaps the most serious. For example, suppose that the net present values for three mutually exclusive alternatives are as follows.

	Alternatives		
	X	Y	Z
Investment.....................	$20,000	$20,000	$20,000
Discounted cash flow	18,000	22,000	25,000
Net present value	(2,000)	2,000	5,000

Obviously X does not meet the required investment rate, while Y and Z do. Between the two of them Z is preferable. But suppose that the alternatives were as follows.

	Alternatives	
	P	Q
Investment	$10,000	$16,000
Discounted Cash Flow	12,000	19,000
Net Present Value	2,000	3,000

Which alternative is preferable? Q has a higher net present value than P but the required investment is also higher. If the projects are mutually exclusive, P is best if money for capital projects is scarce; Q would be taken in the opposite case. But which is best financially? One approach is to calculate the *profitability ratio* by dividing the net present value by the initial investment.

	Alternatives	
	P	Q
Net Present Value	$ 2,000	$ 3,000
Investment	10,000	16,000
Profitability Ratio	20%	18.75%

P has the highest ratio on this basis. One serious problem with this method is that the ratio itself is simply an arbitrary numerical construct; it has no economic meaning and as such is not easily explained. The internal rate of return method partly overcomes this problem.

IV. INTERNAL RATE OF RETURN (Adjusted Rate of Return)

Consider the following example.

Investment	$10,000
After Tax Savings	$ 2,000/year for 10 years (end of year payments)

Now $2,000/year for 10 years discounted at 6% is (7.36 × $2,000) $14,720. At 8%, it is (6.71 × $2,000) $13,420. As the discount rate is increased, the total discounted cash flow is reduced. Obviously, if we keep going higher we will find some rate at which the discounted cash flow is just equal to $10,000. Put another way, there is always some discount rate at which the net present value is zero. This discount rate is called the *internal rate of return* and is shown in Table 8-8.

Table 8-8

Interest rate	After tax savings 1–10 years	Present value factor	Total discounted cash flow
6%	$2,000	7.36	$14,720
8	2,000	6.71	13,420
10	2,000	6.14	12,280
12	2,000	5.65	11,300
14	2,000	5.22	10,440
16	2,000	4.83	9,660
18	2,000	4.49	8,980

The internal rate of return for this project is thus somewhere between 14% and 16%. With more detailed present value tables or a computer we could calculate the exact rate. (It is 15.10%.)

If we had, say, three alternatives, the internal rate of return could be calculated for each. If all three return rates were higher than the company's required earnings rate, all three could be approved. If they were mutually exclusive, that project with the highest adjusted rate of return would be preferred.

Advantages and Disadvantages. This method overcomes the problem of the net present value approach in that a definite return is calculated for each investment alternative and the rates can be compared one to another and to the organization's hurdle rate. A major disadvantage of this method is the complexity of the calculations, which are essentially a process of hunting for a particular discount rate. Computer programs and financial calculators are now readily available to make these calculations, but, as the reader will note, this method is a long way from the simple payback calculation with respect to ease of use.[4]

Perhaps the greatest advantage of the internal rate of return method, at least as compared to net present value, is that it has a simple explanation. In fact, the internal rate of return can be explained without regard to discounting or the time value of money. Take the previous example in which a $10,000 investment yielding $2,000 cash flow for 10 years meant an internal rate of 15.10%. Exactly what does that 15.10% rate of return mean?

If a project has an internal rate of return of 15.10%, sometime over the life of the project the original investment will be repaid (return *of* investment). Further, for each year that some part of the original investment is not repaid (and is still at risk in the project), there will be a payment of 15.10% of the amount still at risk (return *on* investment).

We can prove that this explanation is accurate with the following tabulation, called an amortization table.

Table 8-9 Amortization Table

Year	Investment at risk	Total payment	15.10% Return on investment	Return of investment
1	$10,000	$2,000	$1,510	$ 490
2	9,510	2,000	1,436	564
3	8,946	2,000	1,351	649
...	.	.	.	.
...	.	.	.	.
9	3,247	2,000	490	1,510
10	1,737	2,000	263	1,737

Payment divided between

Thus, during the first year when $10,000 was invested (or was at risk), the return *on* investment is $1,510; this leaves $490 of the total $2,000 payment as a partial return *of* investment. Accordingly, during the second year only $9,510 is at risk, or still invested in the project, and so on. In the last year, the $2,000 payment is just sufficient to return 15.10% *on* the investment still at risk (now $1,737) and to repay the last *of* the investment as well ($1,737). If this process looks suspiciously like a mortgage table, it should, because it is. Indeed, a $10,000 10 year, 15.10% mortgage calling for annual payments only (at year-end) would require a yearly payment of $2,000. That payment stream of $2,000/year would be divided between interest (return *on* investment) and principal (return *of* investment) just as we've done in our amortization table.

---

[4] In one simple case the internal rate of return can be calculated easily—the situation in which after-tax savings are uniform each year. The procedure is to divide the investment by the yearly after-tax savings. The results are then used to find a corresponding interest rate in Tables III and IV at the end of this chapter. For example, in the previous problem,

$$\$10,000/\$2,000 = 5.$$

In Table III for 10 years, 5 falls somewhere between 14% and 16%.

**Considering
Risk**

We have mentioned risk at several points throughout this chapter and have observed several ways in which it might be handled.

1. In addition to the "most likely" forecast of results, a conservative or optimistic schedule may also be studied.

2. Very short payback periods may be required of risky investments. For example, some companies require a small tool replacement investment to have a two-year payback.

3. If one of the return on investment methods is used, different risk categories may be established—each with its own hurdle rate. In one company, product enhancement investments must return 20%, new product investments, 25%; and foreign investments, 40%.

4. Short economic lives may be used to constrain the decision.

While these approaches have merit, they are not as sound as more refined methods. When people discuss risk, what they really mean is the uncertainty of future events and the resulting difficulty in trying to predict the impact of various alternatives. Much work has been done in this area to develop practical approaches to decision making under conditions of uncertainty. While a detailed discussion of these methods is well beyond the scope of this book, the basic approach can be summarized.[5]

Financial theorists generally agree that the best means of dealing with uncertainty lies in trying to establish probabilities of various outcomes of a particular alternative. Instead of "What is the most likely estimate of savings?" we try to determine "What are the chances of the savings being less than $2,000 (say) per month? or $3,000? or $5,000" and so on. Of course it is much more difficult to collect this type of information, particularly when the chances of one thing's happening are related to the chances of something else. Indeed, one of the disadvantages of this approach is the cost and energy which the decision maker must spend to gather the refined predictions. However, with these predictions it is possible to state an answer thus: "the chances of the ROI being below 12% are only 6%; below 15% they are 20%—instead of merely stating the single "most likely" answer. One can see from the following hypothetical results table that a probability answer could provide much more useful information to the decision maker.

---

[5] For further material in this area, the reader is directed to *Probability and Statistics* by Robert Schlaifer, McGraw-Hill Book Company, Inc., 1959.

HYPOTHETICAL	*"Most Likely" Estimate*	*Probability Answer*	
ALTERNATIVE	Internal Rate of Return 12%	*Probability*	*Of a Return Less Than*
		35%	6%
		40	8
		45	10
		55	12
		90	14
		95	16

Here we see that the "most likely" return is 12%. But the formal risk methods yield ROI probabilities showing that chances are great that the return will be less than 12%, while chances are slim that the return will be greater than 12%.

Preparing the Budget

The last step in capital budgeting is to pull together the results of each project evaluation into a set of spending plans for the organization. This process does not mean that the results of each project are automatically included in the capital budget. Sometimes projects are included even if they fail to meet the evaluation criteria. On the other hand, sometimes a project will be deleted from the budget even if it passes the return criteria. Omissions are often made when an organization has more good project ideas than money to fund them all. In other instances, good projects may not be funded because the product or division affected is not in the growth segment of the company's overall strategic plan. In short, evaluating and ranking the proposed project is just part of the capital budgeting process. The final decision will be influenced by long-range strategies, which necessarily affect the validity and importance of individual capital expenditure projects.

SPECIAL TOPICS

Four issues arise so often in capital expenditure evaluations that special comments on each are in order.

Inflation

Present value or discounting does not explicitly incorporate any provision for anticipated price changes or a change in the general level of prices—inflation. At times when future price levels as well as inflation are expected to change, special techniques must be employed to properly evaluate expected project returns. Such techniques involve first the projecting of cash flows based on the prices expected to be obtained during each time period. In other words one must forecast period by period what cash flows one actually expects to realize in dollars of that time period. Then an adjustment to reduce or deflate these cash flows is made, thereby expressing them all in dollars of a common purchasing power usually the starting point or time zero of the project. After the cash flows have been deflated then they are discounted in the normal way to determine an inflation-adjusted or inflation-free rate of return or net present value.[6]

Economic Lives

Typically, a proposed capital expenditure represents an alternative to what will otherwise occur—the so-called status-quo. For the new project to actually be an alternative to the status-quo it is necessary for each to have the same project life or economic life. Otherwise one is not the alternative to the other. Often one faces a situation like the following:

> Suppose the present machine will only last for six more years, and the new, alternative machine will last ten years. This situation can be diagrammed as follows.

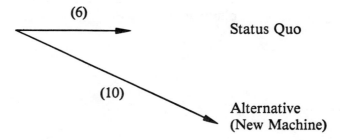

How are these two options to be compared? Actually, there are several ways of handling this. One method is to determine first what the replacement for the old machine would be in six more years, and to incorporate those costs into the cash flows. If the replacement has a life of just four years, the problem is solved as the economic lives are equal as shown below.

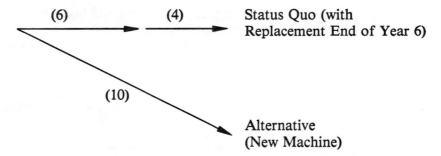

If the replacement machine envisioned in year six has an economic life of, say, eight years, then it might be necessary to determine what the replacement in ten years would be for the new machine and continue this process until the economic lives were equal, as shown below.

---

[6] These techniques are discussed more fully in:

Nichol, David J., "The Impact of Inflation on Present Value Analysis," *Business Economics*, May 1979, pp. 33-38.

Allen, Brandt R., "Evaluating Capital Expenditures Under Inflation: A Primer," *Business Horizons*, December 1976, pp. 30-39.

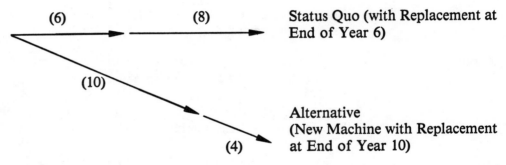

If the economic lives can't quickly be made equal by such a process, adding replacements out into the future becomes impractical. Another means must be used to make the lives equal. Often this is to force the lives to be equal by "cutting the economic life and assessing the residual value." This is diagrammed below.

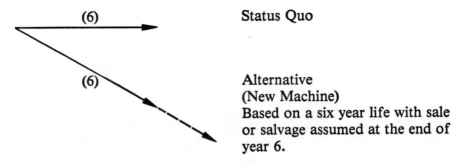

As shown, the cash flows are projected as if the new machine is kept only six years, then sold or scrapped. In effect we're reasoning as follows.

> Our present machine will last six more years, and the alternative is to buy a new one and run it for six years. In six years it still has some remaining life or use which of course is reflected in its sales value or residual value.

We could have forced the economic life somewhere else, as shown below.

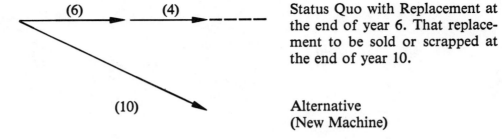

If projects are to be evaluated, they must have finite lives. If one project is really an alternative to another, the lives must be equal. Often, getting the lives equal can only be accomplished by forcing an artificial economic life, which in turn forces a residual value.

**RESIDUAL
VALUES**

All projects have an end; at that time assets are sold or scrapped, working capital is recovered and other costs and revenues are realized. Assessing residual or terminal values is a vital part of the capital expenditure evaluation process. The key question is always: at the project's end what is the cash flow? In some cases it may be negative; for example, it is argued today that the tear down cost for a nuclear power reactor may be greater than its original construction cost. In other instances the residual value may be the opportunity value of an established product or market or even market potential. Often the residual value of a project is the present value of the next or follow-on effort brought about or made possible by the first project. Such values, while quite difficult to assess, are crucial to sound project evaluation.

**PRESENT VALUE
FACTORS AND
TIME FRAMES**

Managers often become confused about whether to use middle-of-year or end-of-year present value factors. The answer depends upon the nature of the cash flows. If the flows occur at fixed points, such as the end of the year or end of a month, then end of year or end of month factors, respectively, should be used. If the flows occur continuously throughout a month or year, as is typical for revenue or cost savings, then middle of the period factors are appropriate. Income taxes present special problems in that for most U.S. companies, they must be estimated in advance and paid quarterly. Tax savings or tax losses, for example, often affect the next immediate tax payment.

APPENDIX: PRESENT VALUE FACTORS

Table I
Present Value of $1 Received at End of Year Indicated

$$P.V. = 1 \div (1 + 1)^n$$

End of Year	2%	4%	6%	8%	10%	12%	14%	16%	18%	20%	25%	30%
1	.98	.96	.94	.93	.91	.89	.88	.86	.85	.83	.80	.77
2	.96	.92	.89	.86	.83	.80	.77	.75	.71	.70	.64	.59
3	.94	.89	.84	.79	.75	.71	.67	.64	.61	.58	.51	.46
4	.93	.86	.79	.73	.68	.63	.59	.55	.52	.48	.41	.35
5	.90	.82	.75	.68	.62	.57	.52	.47	.44	.40	.33	.27
6	.89	.79	.71	.63	.56	.51	.46	.41	.37	.34	.26	.20
7	.87	.76	.66	.59	.51	.45	.40	.36	.31	.28	.21	.16
8	.85	.73	.63	.54	.47	.41	.35	.30	.27	.23	.17	.12
9	.84	.70	.59	.50	.42	.36	.31	.26	.22	.19	.13	.10
10	.82	.68	.56	.46	.39	.32	.27	.23	.19	.16	.11	.07
11	.81	.65	.52	.43	.35	.29	.23	.20	.16	.14	.09	.06
12	.79	.63	.50	.40	.32	.26	.21	.17	.14	.11	.07	.04
13	.77	.60	.47	.37	.29	.23	.18	.14	.12	.09	.05	.03
14	.76	.58	.44	.34	.26	.20	.16	.13	.10	.08	.04	.03
15	.74	.55	.42	.31	.24	.18	.14	.11	.08	.07	.04	.02
20	.67	.45	.31	.22	.15	.10	.07	.05	.04	.03	.01	.01
25	.61	.37	.23	.15	.09	.06	.04	.03	.02	.01	—	—
30	.55	.31	.17	.10	.06	.03	.02	.01	.01	—	—	—
35	.50	.25	.13	.07	.04	.02	.01	.01	—	—	—	—
40	.45	.21	.10	.05	.02	.01	—	—	—	—	—	—

Table II
Present Value of $1 Received at Middle of Year Indicated

$$P.V. = 1 \div (1 + i)^{n-1/2}$$

Middle of Year	2%	4%	6%	8%	10%	12%	14%	16%	18%	20%	25%	30%
1	.99	.98	.97	.96	.95	.95	.94	.93	.92	.91	.89	.88
2	.97	.94	.92	.89	.87	.84	.82	.80	.78	.76	.72	.67
3	.95	.91	.86	.83	.79	.75	.72	.69	.66	.63	.57	.52
4	.93	.87	.82	.76	.72	.67	.63	.60	.56	.53	.46	.40
5	.92	.84	.77	.71	.65	.60	.55	.51	.48	.44	.37	.31
6	.90	.81	.72	.65	.59	.54	.49	.44	.40	.37	.29	.23
7	.88	.77	.69	.61	.54	.48	.43	.38	.34	.31	.23	.18
8	.86	.75	.64	.56	.49	.43	.37	.33	.29	.25	.19	.14
9	.84	.71	.61	.52	.44	.38	.33	.28	.24	.21	.15	.11
10	.83	.69	.58	.48	.40	.34	.29	.25	.21	.18	.12	.08
11	.81	.66	.54	.45	.37	.31	.25	.21	.18	.15	.10	.07
12	.80	.64	.51	.41	.33	.27	.22	.18	.15	.12	.07	.05
13	.78	.61	.48	.38	.30	.24	.20	.15	.12	.10	.06	.04
14	.76	.59	.46	.36	.28	.22	.17	.14	.11	.09	.05	.03
15	.75	.57	.43	.33	.25	.19	.15	.11	.09	.07	.04	.02
20	.68	.47	.32	.22	.16	.11	.08	.05	.04	.03	.01	—
25	.61	.38	.24	.15	.10	.06	.04	.03	.02	.02	—	—
30	.56	.31	.18	.10	.06	.04	.02	.01	.01	.01	—	—
35	.50	.26	.13	.07	.04	.02	.01	.01	—	—	—	—
40	.46	.21	.10	.05	.02	.01	—	—	—	—	—	—

**Table III
Present Value
of $1 Received
at End of Year
for "N" Years**

Period in Years	2%	4%	6%	8%	10%	12%	14%	16%	18%	20%	25%	30%
1	.98	.96	.94	.93	.91	.89	.88	.86	.85	.83	.80	.77
2	1.94	1.88	1.83	1.79	1.74	1.69	1.65	1.61	1.56	1.53	1.44	1.36
3	2.88	2.77	2.67	2.58	2.49	2.40	2.32	2.25	2.17	2.11	1.95	1.82
4	3.81	3.63	3.46	3.31	3.17	3.03	2.91	2.80	2.69	2.59	2.36	2.17
5	4.71	4.45	4.21	3.99	3.79	3.60	3.43	3.27	3.13	2.99	2.69	2.44
6	5.60	5.24	4.92	4.62	4.35	4.11	3.89	3.68	3.50	3.33	2.95	2.64
7	6.47	6.00	5.58	5.21	4.86	4.56	4.29	4.04	3.81	3.61	3.16	2.80
8	7.32	6.73	6.21	5.75	5.33	4.97	4.64	4.34	4.08	3.84	3.33	2.92
9	8.16	7.43	6.80	6.25	5.75	5.33	4.95	4.60	4.30	4.03	3.46	3.02
10	8.98	8.11	7.36	6.71	6.14	5.65	5.22	4.83	4.49	4.19	3.57	3.09
11	9.79	8.76	7.88	7.14	6.49	5.94	5.45	5.03	4.65	4.33	3.66	3.15
12	10.58	9.39	8.38	7.54	6.81	6.20	5.66	5.20	4.79	4.44	3.73	3.19
13	11.35	9.99	8.85	7.91	7.10	6.43	5.84	5.34	4.91	4.53	3.78	3.22
14	12.11	10.57	9.29	8.25	7.36	6.63	6.00	5.47	5.01	4.61	3.82	3.25
15	12.85	11.12	9.71	8.56	7.60	6.81	6.14	5.58	5.09	4.68	3.86	3.27
20	16.35	13.59	11.47	9.82	8.51	7.47	6.62	5.93	5.35	4.87	3.95	3.32
25	19.52	15.62	12.78	10.68	9.08	7.85	6.88	6.09	5.47	4.95	3.99	3.33
30	22.40	17.30	13.76	11.26	9.43	8.06	7.01	6.18	5.52	4.98	4.00	3.33
35	25.00	18.67	14.49	11.65	9.64	8.18	7.07	6.21	5.54	4.99	4.00	3.33
40	27.36	19.80	15.04	11.92	9.78	8.25	7.11	6.23	5.55	5.00	4.00	3.33

**Table IV
Present Value
of $1 Received
at Middle of
Each Year for
"N" Years**

Period in Years	2%	4%	6%	8%	10%	12%	14%	16%	18%	20%	25%	30%
1	.99	.98	.97	.96	.95	.95	.94	.93	.92	.91	.89	.88
2	1.96	1.92	1.89	1.85	1.82	1.79	1.76	1.73	1.70	1.67	1.61	1.55
3	2.91	2.83	2.75	2.68	2.61	2.54	2.48	2.42	2.36	2.30	2.18	2.07
4	3.84	3.70	3.57	3.44	3.33	3.21	3.11	3.02	2.92	2.83	2.64	2.47
5	4.76	4.54	4.34	4.15	3.98	3.81	3.66	3.53	3.40	3.27	3.01	2.78
6	5.66	5.35	5.06	4.80	4.57	4.35	4.15	3.97	3.80	3.64	3.30	3.01
7	6.54	6.12	5.75	5.41	5.11	4.83	4.58	4.35	4.14	3.95	3.53	3.19
8	7.40	6.87	6.39	5.97	5.60	5.26	4.95	4.68	4.43	4.20	3.72	3.33
9	8.24	7.58	7.00	6.49	6.04	5.64	5.28	4.96	4.67	4.41	3.87	3.44
10	9.07	8.27	7.58	6.97	6.44	5.98	5.57	5.21	4.88	4.59	3.99	3.52
11	9.88	8.93	8.12	7.42	6.81	6.29	5.82	5.42	5.06	4.74	4.09	3.59
12	10.68	9.57	8.63	7.83	7.14	6.56	6.04	5.60	5.21	4.86	4.16	3.64
13	11.46	10.18	9.11	8.21	7.44	6.80	6.24	5.75	5.33	4.96	4.22	3.68
14	12.22	10.77	9.57	8.57	7.72	7.02	6.41	5.89	5.44	5.05	4.27	3.71
15	12.97	11.34	10.00	8.90	7.97	7.21	6.56	6.00	5.53	5.12	4.31	3.73
20	16.51	13.86	11.81	10.20	8.93	7.91	7.07	6.38	5.81	5.33	4.42	3.78
25	19.72	15.93	13.16	11.09	9.52	8.30	7.34	6.56	5.94	5.42	4.45	3.80
30	22.62	17.64	14.18	11.70	9.88	8.53	7.48	6.65	5.99	5.46	4.46	3.80
35	25.25	19.04	14.93	12.11	10.11	8.66	7.55	6.69	6.02	5.47	4.46	3.80
40	27.63	20.19	15.50	12.39	10.26	8.73	7.58	6.71	6.03	5.48	4.47	3.80

part
four

management control

INTRODUCTION   Control is the process by which management assures itself that the organization's resources are used effectively and efficiently in pursuit of the organization's objectives. Stated another way, it is the procedure, either formal or informal, by which a manager sees to it that "things are going the way he or she wants"; that is, that equipment and other assets are used wisely, that employees are properly motivated, that funds are expended carefully, that materials are not wasted, and that, in general, all resources (assets, people, money, time, ideas) are directed toward the organization's goals. In a very small organization, the control system is informal because by personal observation, inspection and direct involvement in decision making the ex-

127

ecutive can ensure that all resources are properly managed. In larger organizations control is achieved through a more formal system that often involves accounting reports, budgets, standards, performance measures, as well as informal supervision. Although non-financial measures are sometimes used and are often very important, management control systems usually are based upon financial information. They typically contain two elements: planning or budgeting activity which is followed by after-the-fact data collection and report preparation. These reports usually compare actual results to planned performance, and lead to some type of performance measure or measures. For example, during the early 1960's the General Electric Company was divided into over 100 decentralized departments. Each department was evaluated by the same four performance indicators: (1) profitability, (2) market position, (3) productivity, and (4) product leadership. For each of these indicators a specific, detailed measurement was developed and was made a part of the planning, budgeting, and reporting system of each division.

CONTROL RATIONALE

While developing and applying measurements are the tangible parts of this process, the underlying purpose for any management control system is to motivate and direct *people*. Organizations consist primarily of people who make decisions about allocations of resources, direction of activity, intensity of effort, and the like; consequently, it is these people who must be motivated to take action and make the kinds of decisions that lead to the organization's goals. Too many people have been misled into thinking that control is an after-the-fact mechanism because it involves measuring results, comparing them to a budget or plan, and then taking corrective action if results do not conform to plan. Some authors have even proposed the electrical engineers' "feedback loop" as a model of the management control process. While control does involve these steps, it also entails much more. After-the-fact action can never change a bad decision or save wasted time, materials, and effort because by definition such actions are too late. The only effective method of control is to influence the decision maker in advance of his decision. This is where motivation and direction come in. We achieve effective control only when the decision maker knows in advance what is expected of him and how his performance will be judged, and when, because of this knowledge, he is encouraged to act in a manner consistent with the company's objectives. This motivation and direction through measurement is the essence of management control.

9

Management
Control Systems

A firm's management control system is actually a collection of integrated subsystems or building blocks that together provide the formal means by which top management actually runs the business. These subsystems are

1. Organizational structure—responsibility centers.

2. Measures of performance.

3. Planning and budgeting.

4. Capital budgeting.

5. Managerial rewards and punishment.

Organizational design is one of the basic building blocks of control because it reflects the division of resources and the assignment of responsibility throughout the firm. In particular, each organizational unit headed by a manager can be considered a responsibility center. Responsibility centers vary from the simple budget or cost centers widely used in manufacturing companies to the sophisticated profit and return on investment centers found in decentralized divisions of large multinational companies.

The actual measures of performance used in a responsibility center are generally unique quantitative formulations designed especially for that unit, division, or group. For example, a profit center's primary measure of performance is of course profit, but in a particular division profit could be further defined as profit exclusive of inter-company sales, before material price variances, after allocation of budgeted corporate general and administrative expense (allocated on the basis of budgeted gross sales), before federal and state income taxes but after excise and local real estate taxes, and so on. In some companies, such as GE, a basic set of carefully designed measures is used throughout the corporation; in others, standardized measures are used only within a group or division.

The planning and budgeting system of the firm is also an integral part of its management control. Through it, various levels of management communiate their expectations, commitments, judgments, and estimates. Another part of the planning and budgeting system is that set of procedures used to generate, screen, evaluate, and budget capital expenditures. Management control also includes executive compensation systems and other rewards and punishments, since these devices also motivate and direct personnel.

ORGANIZATIONAL DESIGN AND RESPONSIBILITY CENTERS

For purposes of this discussion, a "responsibility center" will be defined as any organizational unit headed by a person assigned a specific responsibility. The unit might be one of the departments of a factory, a group of departments, the whole plant, or perhaps the division. Responsibility centers are to be found in all parts of a company from manufacturing and sales to research and administration. Whatever its size, location, or perceived importance, if the unit is a part of the organization, if it has been assigned certain responsibilities, and if it is directed or managed by someone charged with those responsibilities, it is a responsibility center.

For control purposes, an organization's structure is best viewed as a hierarchical assembly of responsibility centers, of which there are five basic types, as depicted in Figure 9-1. Each type has its own control function and means of measurement.

**Figure 9-1
Type of
Responsibility
Center**

	Standard Cost	Discretionary Expense	Revenue	Profit	Investment
Information Required	Costs Incurred, Resources Used, Production or Service Levels, Standards	Expenses	Revenue	Revenue, Costs and Expenses	Revenue, Costs and Expenses, Assets Employed
Primary Measure	Variances or Costs/Unit	Expenses: Actual vs. Budget	Revenue: Actual vs. Quota	Profit: Actual vs. Budget	Return on Investment or Residual Income: Actual vs. Budget
Primary Objective	Cost Minimization	Spending Constraints	Revenue Maximization	Profit Maximization	Profit Optimization Relative to Assets Employed

**Standard
Cost
Centers**

Cost centers collect information on resources used and compare these actual costs to the standards allowed for the level of goods produced or services rendered. Typical measures of performance for a cost center would be

Example	*Measure*
Factory Work Center	Variances such as labor efficiency, material usage, scrappage, or overhead spending.
Oil Refinery	Cost/barrel vs. standard.
Bank Operations Center	Cost/check handled vs. standard.
Trucking Company	Cost/mile vs. standard.

A hallmark of both cost centers and expense centers is that no attempt is made to attribute revenue to them or to measure the value of services provided in financial terms. Cost centers, however, do measure the amount of output or service produced and either express the results in terms of cost/unit or contrast actual costs with standard or with some other measure of what should have been spent to generate that amount of output.

Not all standard cost centers actually use formal standard cost accounting. Instead, the actual cost per unit may be derived and used to monitor performance by comparing actual to either standard cost or historical average. For example, hospitals, trucking companies, airlines, food processors, and mining and manufacturing companies often calculate average cost per unit on a periodic basis and compare it to previous period without using any formal standard cost. The necessary ingredients for standard cost centers are

1. Ability to measure the actual resources used, such as materials, labor, and overhead.

2. Ability to measure or count the output or services produced.

3. A predetermined standard cost or cost allowance or historical base.

**Discretionary
Expense
Centers**

Expense centers are typically used for administrative departments; this type of responsibility center control permits or authorizes spending up to a predetermined (budget) level. These budgets are generally established in advance and do not vary with departmental activity or output; that is, normally they do not "flex." Indeed, the actual results or outputs of discretionary expense centers are not even measured, often because of the difficulties of doing so. For example, the accounting department of a company is usually treated as an expense center. Actual expenses are collected and compared to budget; neither the value nor the quantity of the department's output is measured.

No doubt the major difference between standard cost centers and discretionary expense centers is the former's ability to measure results. We use standard cost centers when it's possible to measure the outputs produced and to prescribe what should be the costs of such output. Because this is not possible with discretionary expense centers, their budgets cannot be considered statements of what should have been spent. Consequently, overspending in discretionary expense centers isn't necessarily bad nor underspending good. The legal department's budget for example cannot be considered a statement of "what should be spent" for legal services; as a consequence, one cannot interpret a comparison of budgeted and actual expenditures as a measure of efficiency in these situations.

Revenue Centers

This type of responsibility center is appropriate for many marketing and sales units where the primary mission is to generate revenue. Such units always incur expenses as well (salaries, office expense, travel, advertising, etc.), but control emphasis is not directed to cost minimization but to revenue maximization. As a general rule, all revenue centers have expense budgets as well, but these really serve as spending constraints. Revenue center control thus accomplishes two objectives: it prescribes the level of resources the manager may spend, and it directs the manager to maximize revenues subject to this constraint.

Revenue in these situations is not necessarily measured in the same way as for general accounting purposes. Orders received may be measured rather than sales billed; inter-company sales may be at some price other than market; commissions may be measured rather than sales dollars; sales or revenues might be weighted to encourage a desired sales mix.

Profit Centers

A profit center is any responsibility center where both expenses and revenues are attributed to the center and where the manager is expected to make trade-offs between the two in order to increase the net difference or profit. The chief difference between profit and revenue centers lies in the trade-off between expense and revenue: the revenue center manager does not make these trade-offs; the profit center manager does. Decentralized divisions of large manufacturing companies are often measured as profit centers. Individual plants within a company might be profit centers; so might the various units of a hospital, such as intensive care or emergency room.

The distinction between an expense or cost center and a profit center is not whether the results or outputs of the unit *can* be measured in terms of revenue, but whether they *are*. In one of the large U.S. container companies, all of the can and bottle plants are treated as cost centers—at a competitor, the plants are profit centers.

Whether a center should be a profit center or an expense center depends on several factors. If revenue is not measurable or attributable to the center, the unit should not be a profit center. How much control or influence the center's manager has over prices or volume is also important. If a plant has no marketing responsibility and cannot otherwise influence the volume sold or the price, then controlling it as a profit center seems pointless. Unless the actual profit performance is adjusted to remove the influence of any changes in sales volume, price, and mix from budget, the performance measure is distorted by many factors beyond the manager's control. Yet if all of these adjustments are made, the profit center becomes really an expense center.

Control in a profit center is usually accomplished through a budget—in this case a profit budget. Profit centers are ordinarily not compared one to another within the firm because each usually has a different profit potential. This is why budgeting is so important. If a plant's profit is to be compared to its budgeted profit and the manager's performance judged accordingly, the effectiveness of the system is directly related to the quality of the budget. If the budget is a fair, meaningful target, representing real accomplishment, and if the budget is so accepted by the manager, then the control system can be a powerful instrument for directing and motivating managers. But if the budgets are "soft" or arbitrary or impossible to achieve, then the profit control mechanism will be ineffective.

Another factor influencing control systems that use profit centers is *transfer pricing*. Whenever two profit centers within an organization trade with each other, the internal selling price (or transfer price) becomes very important to both responsibility centers. The buying price of one is the selling price of the other. An integrated oil company might set up the oil producing properties as one profit center and the refinery and marketing divisions as two more. Clearly, a transfer price must be established for each grade of product and between each division. However, this is often difficult to do. A few examples should illustrate this point. If the transfer price between the refinery and the marketing division is too low, the refinery may be encouraged to sell its product elsewhere or to change its production mix to yield a more profitable range of products. The low price to the marketing division might also encourage wasteful price cutting. If the price is set too high, the refinery may switch its production the other way, while the marketing division may be prevented from bidding on a special deal that, while a loss to the marketing division at that price, would really be beneficial to the company as a whole.

The complexity of a transfer pricing situation depends upon the number of profit centers; the degree of trading among them; the number of different products; the frequency of changes in costs, in production volume, and in external market prices and demands; the amount of joint or by-products; and the importance of "good" transfer prices. It is not unusual for an organization to commit a large group of people to the continual task of establishing and revising the transfer pricing mechanisms.

**Investment
Centers**

An investment center is any responsibility center whose costs and expenses, revenue, and asset investment are all attributed to the center. All three figures are combined into a single measure of performance. The most frequent measure used is Return on Investment: net income of the responsibility unit is divided by the unit's assets, which is considered to be the company's investment in that unit. In some cases only inventory and accounts receivable are included in the investment base; in other situations land, buildings and equipment, and even cash are included. Current liabilities such as accounts payable and accrued expenses are sometimes deducted thus resulting in a figure normally termed *net assets*. In such instances the ROI is often called RONA for Return on Net Assets. ROI, RONA, ROA (Return on Assets) and ROCE (Return on Capital Employed) are simply variations in terminology for the primary measure of performance used in an investment center.

The impact that changing the investment center measure has on the manager's motivation can easily be shown. If inventory is part of the investment base and the manager is currently earning 10% ROI, every additional dollar of inventory must "earn" at least 10% plus the additional cost of handling the inventory, or the manager's performance measure will decline. If inventory is not included in the investment base, then each extra $1.00 of inventory need only cover its carrying cost. To improve performance above 10% ROI, every asset that earns less than 10% and can be scrapped or sold, should be.

The relationship between the capital budgeting system and management control through investment centers is also clear. A division earning 15% ROI can only hurt itself by proposing capital investment projects that earn 12 or 13%. What may not be so clear is that if several divisions are all earning at different rates, as is usually the case, the discrepancies may have a disastrous impact on the capital budgeting system. Consider the following situation.

Division	ROI Earning Rate
A	4%
B	12
C	25

The company as a whole earns 15% ROI, but each of the three divisions has a different ROI. In this situation, where will all of the capital funds go? To the C division? Not likely! In the eyes of C, "good" projects must earn at least 25%. C's managers are motivated to spurn 20% return alternatives because C's performance measure, ROI, will necessarily go down, even though a 20% return project will improve total company ROI. At the other extreme, 5, 6, and 7% return projects, while falling well below the average company ROI, look very attractive to Division A. Unless the capital budgeting system has been designed to thwart this tendency, Division A may request funds for just these projects. Since there are always many more low return ideas than high ones, Division A may very well end up with the bulk of new capital funds. As these examples indicate, the design of investment center performance measures should be carefully related to the capital budgeting system.[1]

---

[1] Relating the expected return on capital expenditures to the ROI of a responsibility center is much more complicated than is suggested by these simple examples. ROI performance for an investment center is an accounting measure often exclusive of income taxes whereas ROI as used in capital budgeting is normally either a net present value or the internal rate of return measure, derived from applying present value techniques to estimated future cash flows, almost always on an after tax basis. Indeed, ROI as applied to historical performance of an investment center and ROI as used in capital budgeting are rarely comparable. (The only exception is when a firm uses the unadjusted rate of return method, as explained in Chapter 8, for evaluating capital expenditures. This too is often called ROI.) Because ROI is used by many executives to refer to both historical accounting results and to prospective cash flows, great care must be exercised to avoid confusion.

An alternative approach, designed to eliminate this problem, measures *residual income* or RI, which is computed in the following manner:

$$\text{Residual Income} = \text{Profit} - (\text{capital charge}) \times \text{Investment}.$$

For example, suppose that a division has $100 million of investment (inventory, receivables, land, buildings, and equipment), profit for the year of $30 million, and a corporate charge for assets of 15%. While ROI would be 30/100 or 30%, RI is calculated thus:

$$\text{RI} = 30 - (.15)\,100 = 15 \text{ or } \$15 \text{ million.}$$

Residual income has several advantages over ROI. First, because it is a dollar figure rather than a ratio, a manager is not motivated to increase his performance measure by decreasing total investment. Secondly, coordinating the capital budgeting system's required rate of return with the capital charge used for RI makes the two systems compatible. Under RI measurement, a high-earning division, such as in this example, is motivated to invest in projects below 30% but above 15%. Likewise, a lower-earning division will only invest in projects expected to earn better than 15%. It is also possible to use different charge rates for different classes of assets, that is, 20% for equipment or 8% for inventory.

Accounting for investment centers presents a number of questions whether one uses ROI or RI. Some of the most serious include

1. Should a share of corporate cash be "assigned" to the responsibility center?

2. Should accounts receivable be included in the investment base if the corporation operates a centralized billing, collections, and payment system?

3. Should inventories be valued at LIFO, FIFO, or average costs; at market value or at replacement cost?

4. Should the value of land be attributed to the investment center?

5. Should buildings and equipment be included at original cost, book value, replacement cost, or market value?

It is only a slight exaggeration to say that there are as many ways to calculate ROI or RI as there are companies using the investment center form of control.

Business typically employ several different types of responsibility center measures in different parts of the organization. For example, a company may treat the various manufacturing departments within its plants as cost centers, while the plants may be judged as profit centers. At the same time the company could be treating the sales regions as revenue centers, the administrative departments as expense centers, and perhaps the major product divisions of the company as investment centers.

MEASURES OF PERFORMANCE

Measurements are the heart of management control. How a manager is measured strongly influences the decisions he makes and how he spends his time.

Many companies attempt to separate the performance evaluation of an operating unit (and the measurements used to do it) from the performance evaluation of the individual managers involved. In practice, this is most difficult to do, since the manager in question is responsible for the business unit. In general, it is necessary to decouple the two evaluations to allow for uncontrollable factors, such as economic conditions that bear on the results of the unit. This separation acknowledges in the manager's evaluation that the operating unit's original budget might not be the best set of figures for *ex post facto* managerial evaluation. However, it is unwise to evaluate managers on fundamentally different *measures* of performance from those used for the operating unit. This discrepancy creates conflicts in the manager's mind that weaken his or her overall motivation.

CAPITAL BUDGETING

As discussed in the previous chapter, the capital budgeting system is that process whereby an organization determines how its capital or funds are to be invested to realize increased profits or savings in the future. The capital budget reflects the long-range plans of an organization and is the stated means of implementing those plans. Capital budgeting and management control systems are closely related. First of all, managers and their subordinates must be motivated to search for new ideas, to improve their performance; secondly, capital expenditure is one method that managers may use to improve their performance—they may buy new labor-saving machines, for example. Thirdly, the evaluation and implementation of new capital projects is another management responsibility. The manager's skill at choosing and enacting capital projects should be included in his or her performance measure.

In developing capital budgeting systems, many problems of control may arise. In most cases, the manager who evaluates and proposes a project is the same manager who stands to benefit or be hurt by it. A new machine may save money and improve plant profitability—but perhaps the savings are not quite high enough to justify the purchase to top management, so the savings are "adjusted" ever so slightly, and the project is approved. Conflicts of interest may also work the other way. A project may be very good for the company as a whole because of its long-range potential. But if it will mean heavy losses for the first several years, the division that uncovered this new opportunity may be reluctant to propose it, because that division will have to bear the losses while the project is getting off the ground.

**REWARD AND
PUNISHMENT**

The executive incentive and reward systems of an organization are essential to management control because both are intended to provide motivation. Sometimes the two systems are directly related, as when bonuses or other incentives are tied to performance measures. Unfortunately, the two systems sometimes work at cross purposes. For example, Company X provides a bonus to all plant managers whose plants earn a profit for the year. The bonus is equal to 5% of all profits in excess of budgeted profit up to a maximum bonus of $20,000. At first glance this may appear to be a good incentive plan, for it motivates plant managers to make a profit and to exceed their budgets. However, for the company in question it was a very poor plan. First of all, the overall management control system emphasized return on investment, not just profit. Secondly, the stipulation that only those plants earning a profit were eligible meant that several plants, where even a tight budget reflected an expected loss, were ineligible—even though meeting the budget would still have represented good performance on the part of the manager. Thirdly, placing the bonus on the difference between actual profit and budgeted profit put as much pressure on plant managers to budget low as it did to produce efficiently. Finally, limiting the bonus to $20,000 only served to dampen the enthusiasm of managers once they approached or exceeded the limit. In fact, they might have been motivated to hold back and "save" something for next year (perhaps a cost saving idea, a new product, or a special customer).

As we can see from this example, the compensation system must be carefully related to the management control system to insure proper motivation. Any conflicts between the two systems can cause mixed signals to be transmitted back to the manager.

**TYPES OF
COSTS**

Managers of all five kinds of responsibility centers will be concerned with control of costs. This is particularly true for cost and expense centers where inputs are the primary measure of performance, but also applies to profit and investment centers, for costs are part of the performance goals and measures there also.

Earlier chapters defined costs as direct or indirect, variable or fixed. Costs can also be classified in another way to focus on certain characteristics important to sound expense controls. Three categories are ordinarily used:

1.   Engineered costs.

2.   Managed costs.

3.   Commited costs.

1.   *Engineered costs* are, by definition, those cost elements for which it is possible to determine or prescribe "what the cost should be" for a unit of output or a given level of activity. Thus, in a manufacturing operation where time studies, work methods, and the like have enabled the development of

standard costs or standard times, a system of manufacturing cost control can be employed such that actual expenses are compared to "standard" or "allowed" expense, and a deviation or "variance" is calculated. Engineered costs are not restricted to the factory. Many office operations, such as typing, key-punching, and filing, can be standardized. Standard costs are also used for meals in hospitals and other institutions.

2. *Managed costs or discretionary costs* are by definition the opposite of engineered costs. For these costs it is just not possible to prescribe "what the proper costs should be" for a certain amount of output or for a given result. Consequently, one cannot say whether actual spending was too high or too low. How much should the public relations department spend? the research lab? the computer center? the maintenance department? the accounting department? How much should a hospital spend on housekeeping? Managed-cost expense centers often exist because some important output factor is either too difficult or too expensive to measure. But does this mean that managed costs cannot be controlled? Fortunately, the answer is no. There are means for controlling such costs, but not to the same degree or with the same precision as engineered costs.

One of the most effective means of controlling managed costs is a budget. Preparing and defending a budget forces managers of discretionary expense centers to scrutinize their operations and carefully plan their expenditures. In addition, knowing that spending will be tabulated and compared to budget causes managers to concern themselves with spending, particularly if they know that they will be questioned about any significant differences from the budget. There is still no way to determine which budget level is the "right" one, or whether actual results above or below budget are good or bad, but at least managers are forced to be careful and to plan. The mere fact that managers know someone is watching their spending provides some degree of control—however slim it may be.

Comparison is another means of control. Comparisons with last year, with other organizations, or with industry trends all provide useful information for assessing performance. Furthermore, many organizational policies help managed cost control: policies on job classifications, salary levels, hiring practices, travel allowances, telephone and telegraph usage, etc.

Despite budgets and comparisons, managed costs are not controllable with the mathematical approach that is applicable to engineered costs. One must always remember that the managed expense is one that just cannot be quantifiably judged as "too high" or "too low." Many control system failures can be traced to expense center control systems that treat managed costs as if they were engineered costs, using standards and preset budgets.

3. *Committed costs* are fixed, pre-determined, allocated, or protected from cost cutting. Examples include depreciation, certain contractual items, allocated costs from other departments, and perhaps certain personnel costs. Also included might be "strategic" items such as maintenance, training, and development costs, which are to be segregated from operating costs and protected. Westinghouse, for example, segregates the costs of certain strategic

projects in cost and profit centers to insure that operating managers are not tempted to cut into these areas to compensate for cost overruns or revenue shortfalls in operations. Otherwise such projects tend to be the first place a manager looks for cost savings since they often result in long-term as opposed to immediate benefits.

In some companies, committed costs are considered non-controllable and are excluded from the performance measure. In others, they are included to give the manager "the whole picture"; the manager may have some indirect control or influence over these costs. Arguments for excluding such items center on the notion that "people should not be held accountable for things they don't control." Arguments on the other side sound like "what harm does it do" and "maybe if we leave it in they'll find a way to do something about it.

The dividing lines between these cost categories are often difficult to draw. Also, the nature of a particular cost element changes depending upon the time frame under consideration. "All costs are fixed in the short run and variable in the long run," or so the saying goes. For example, computer rental is pretty much a committed cost on a monthly basis—but viewed over a one- or two-year period it becomes much more controllable (or variable) and hence a managed cost. The time span of control is very important to the design of a control system. These subtleties make designing control systems more an art than a science.

CONTROL SYSTEM DESIGN AND EVALUATION   There are no "generally accepted accounting principles" for designing and evaluating a management control system. The process can perhaps best be viewed as consisting of five steps:

1. Determining goals and objectives of the company.

2. Identifying organizational constraints.

3. Identifying key success variables for each responsibility center.

4. Applying evaluation criteria.

5. Testing and recommending change.

Each of these steps will be discussed in this section.

1. *Determining goals and objectives.* As we noted earlier, management control is goal-oriented. Without a specific statement of objectives, little can be done in the way of evaluation or improvement. Determining the organization's goals is often the most difficult and certainly the most important step. These goals must be expressed so that they aid decision making. Frequently, the organization has multiple objectives. For example, the objectives of a business might be maximizing long-run profit, being a "good employer,"

and being a "good corporate citizen." Unfortunately such a statement leaves much to be desired. Beyond a certain point "being a good employer" may interfere with maximizing profits. Where is that point? Being a "good corporate citizen" may mean that the company is willing to fight pollution, but this too may run counter to profit maximization beyond a certain level of expenditure. Top management should make every effort to refine these objectives so that their meaning is clear.

2. *Identifying organizational constraints.* Once the objectives have been determined, the next step is to study the organizational hierarchy to understand the various organizational relationships and to isolate any significant constraints. For example, in the review of the control system of a large manufacturing company, it was noted that while there were five plants located throughout the country, there were seven sales districts. Furthermore, the areas served by the plants did not match any of the sales territories. The sales managers and the plant managers did not report to the same people. In this case, it was obvious that changing the sales territories or the reporting hierarchy might improve the control system. For instance, one might wish to restructure the sales territories along plant lines, assigning each plant and sales manager in an area to a single manager and making the resulting responsibility area a profit center. If such changes could not be made, the existing structure might be an important constraint on control.

Examining the organizational structure for possible constraints is usually the second step because it sets the limits within which the control system designer must operate. Typically, organizational relationships are given; the management control system must be made to fit them.

3. *Identifying key success variables.* Every responsibility center has a limited number of key tasks or functions critical to the organization's objectives. Identifying these key success variables can often improve the control system as much as anything else the system designer does. Key success variables include such items as cost control, quality, service, sales volume, price, mix, and asset control.

Key success variables are not always measurable, but this is not important. What is important is that the system designer understands enough about the operation of each responsibility center to be able to isolate the key variables so that provision may be made for them in the control system design. The danger of omission at this step is clear: a critical variable or task that is excluded from the system may be ignored rather than emphasized. The key success variables of a manufacturing operation may be (1) on-time delivery, (2) low cost, (3) high quality, in that order. But if an expense center control system is implemented with no provision for measuring product quality or on-time delivery, then these two key factors may be jeopardized. Indeed, a tight expense budget may motivate the plant manager to cut quality and to increase the length of production runs in spite of delays in delivery. If the key success variables are not all considered in the performance measure or measures, then managers won't be motivated to include them all as part of their decision criteria. If, as so often happens, the key variables conflict or represent trade-offs, and some variables are ignored by the performance system, then the decision maker will not only ignore those variables but also may take actions directly opposed to those factors.

4. *Applying evaluation criteria.* Once the objectives have been determined, the structural constraints specified, and the key success variables identified, then the existing or proposed control system may be judged or tested to determine its effectiveness. This evaluation may include some or all of the following criteria.

A. *Goal Congruence.* This is by far the most important test of a control system. The key question here is, "does the proposed performance measure always encourage the manager to take action in the best interest of the organization as a whole?" In other words, will the manager, when acting in his or her own best interest by trying to maximize his or her performance measure, always take those actions or make those decisions that best lead to the organization's objectives? Usually, this test of goal congruence can be applied in a rigorous manner. For example, in the earlier discussion leading to Residual Income the C Division's ROI performance measure encouraged that division to ignore projects with less than 25% return, even though the division might pass up opportunities that were desirable for the company as a whole. Clearly, no one wants that division to ignore 23% return projects. But, by using ROI as a performance measure, the company essentially tells the division manager to do so. Top management might say that its division managers always recognize such conflicts and tend to do what is best for the company as a whole. This may be true, but not all situations are as obvious as this one, and there can be no doubt that the division may easily take certain actions that benefit the division, but harm the overall corporation.

Developing a performance measure congruent with the organization's goals can be very difficult. Consider the company with goals of profitability, growth, and public service, operating 27 manufacturing plants throughout the United States. Each plant was measured as a profit center, and the plant manager's bonus depended upon the degree to which he or she exceeded the profit budget. In 1969, top management installed electrostatic precipitators on the stacks of some of the plants. Senior executives, of course, expected that the precipitators would reduce air pollution. They were very upset when they discovered that plant managers were turning off the precipitators to save the heavy electrical expense involved. To the plant manager, hard pressed to meet budget, the large saving from shutting off the precipitators was a very real temptation. And if the manager didn't wish to risk cutting them during the daylight hours, the precipitators could always be cut at night. Now such cost cutting was clearly not what senior executives had in mind, but they encouraged such action by the profit center system. Correcting this dysfunctional motivation was no easy task. Simply decreasing each plant's profit target by the amount of the expected electrical expense was no solution—for the manager was still motivated to shut off the device.

B. *Feasibility*. Is the proposed system practical or does it cost more to operate than the benefits it provides? The hospital housekeeping problem mentioned earlier is a good example. In that case, it might just be possible to measure the effect of the cleaning operation on sanitation or appearance scales. But the total cost of doing so would undoubtedly be much greater than any savings that could be realized through more "tightly controlled" housekeeping.

C. *Controllability*. "Managers ought not to be held accountable for factors over which they have no control." In control systems, this saying means that the performance measure ought to include at least all of the key success variables of the responsibility center, without being unduly influenced by other factors beyond the manager's influence. Thus, plants whose managers have no marketing or volume responsibility are usually controlled as expense centers. A profit measure might indicate performance above budget only because sales volume went up at a time when manufacturing efficiency, the only factor really under the influence of the manager, was poor. At the other extreme, profits may be down because of a sales slump, yet the manufacturing efficiency may be above standard. Obviously, the profit measure in this situation does not capture the factors under the manager's control.

D. *Understandability*. Managers cannot be motivated by measures they do not understand. Furthermore, by "understand" we mean that the manager appreciates how each decision he makes will affect the measure. Suppose that in the case of the oil company discussed earlier both the refinery and the marketing division were measured as profit centers and that a sizable bonus was given to division management for performance in excess of budget. Suppose, too, that the transfer price for products between the refinery and the marketing division was to be determined at the end of each year (for that year) by taking the average wholesale price during the year for the country as a whole, minus 3%. Now his performance measure is easily explained and its calculation readily understood, but it is not a measure that tells managers of either division how they may improve performance. Because the refinery does not know the transfer price until the year is over, it cannot determine the optimum mix of products. Marketing has a similar problem. The system is easily explained but not easily understood.

E. *Fairness*. Fairness is included on this list of criteria only because it is often considered important by many organizations. *By itself*, there is no logical reason for it. Whether a particular measure is fair or not is of little consequence to success of a control system, other things being equal. A plant manager may be given a budget or target that he or she considers "unfair." But if the performance measure is congruent with the organization's objectives, meets the other criteria and properly motivates the manager, then the control system works whether the manager thinks it is fair or not. But if a system is *so* unfair that managers drop out or cease to strive, then of course the system has failed. Perhaps the best way to say this is that we don't want control systems so unfair as to impair the manager's direction and motivation.

F.   *Long-Run — Short-Run Balance*. Unless designers are careful, a control system may tend to encourage current performance at the expense of future prospects. In fact, this is a continual problem faced by all organizations. Plant maintenance may be cut by the manager desperately trying to meet a tight budget. Research into projects with 5- and 10-year paybacks just won't be undertaken by a division manager who may not keep his or her job even three months unless profits are up.

The other five items on this list are of a nature that one can determine whether the criteria is met or not; that is, a control system is either goal congruent or it is not. Unfortunately, this is not the case with the long-run — short-run balance problem. Here there is no way to determine logically what degree or balance between short-run and long-run emphasis is correct. One can only continually question the balance as the existing control system is reviewed or a new one proposed and tested.

5. *Testing and Recommending Change*. Good management control systems are developed only over a period of time. Since organizational structures, relationships, and constraints are continually changing, since organizational goals are often revised, and since environmental factors often fluctuate, continuous review of management control systems is mandatory. Sometimes new systems are developed by trial and error. More often, a new system is developed when the old one is evaluated because of some apparent weakness, or just because a review is overdue. The evaluation follows the steps outlined above. Before being implemented, the proposed system is tested and its expected results again evaluated. By this repetitive process—evaluate, propose, evaluate, propose—a new system is eventually designed.

A word of warning: control systems cannot compensate for poor management. In this chapter we have stressed the technical aspects of the management control system (the budgets, standards, reports, and measurements), but these are only part of the control process. The system must also be administered by competent managers. Good managers can very often overcome the shortcomings of a weak control system, but the very best control methods are ineffective in the hands of incompetent management.

10

The Impact of Inflation on Business Decisions

Inflation has two primary effects on business decisions:

1. Inflation increases a firm's need for funds to support operations. This is true even if a firm is not expanding its activity.

2. Inflation causes traditional accounting methods to give misleading signals about the profits of a firm or of a product or service. Since many decisions are based at least in part on the profitability of alternative courses of action, inflation may seriously distort the results of traditional approaches to decision making.

    To examine specifically the effects of inflation let us consider a simple illustration.

WIDGET TRADING COMPANY, LTD.   The Widget Trading Company, Ltd. (WTC), buys and sells widgets. Through its longstanding knowledge of the widget market, WTC Ltd. is usually able to sell widgets at twice the price it pays for them. Not all of this 50% margin is profit, however, for WTC incurs some handling expense. In recent years profit has been about 10% on the owners' investment, and the owners have made a practice of returning all the profit to themselves in dividends.

WTC operates in a country whose inflation rate has been around 20% per year, and WTC has found that its purchase costs and selling prices have also been rising about 20% per year. WTC's president decided to look ahead a few years and asked his accountant to forecast sales and profits for the next three years. Exhibit 1 presents the accountant's projection, together with a glimpse of the eleventh year ahead.

According to this projection, WTC will start in year 1 with $50 (or $50 thousand or $50 million), buy 50 widgets at $1.00 each, sell them later for $2.00 each, and incur $45 in expenses. The profit of $5, will be paid out in dividends. (We'll disregard taxes in this example.) In year 2 the cost of widgets will go up 20%, so the firm will buy 41, sell them later, and make its usual 10% return on equity.

Exhibit 10-1

WIDGET TRADING COMPANY LTD.
The Accountant's Forecast
(in thousands or millions of dollars)

	Year 1		Year 2		Year 3		Year 11
Balance Sheet	*Begin*	*End*	*Begin*	*End*	*Begin*	*End*	*Begin*
Cash	$50	$50	$50	$50	$50	$50	$50
Inventory	0	0	0	0	0	0	0
Total assets	$50	$50	$50	$50	$50	$50	$50
Liabilities	0	0	0	0	0	0	0
Owners equity	50	50	50	50	50	50	50
Total L+OE	$50	$50	$50	$50	$50	$50	$50
Cost per widget	$1.00		$1.20		$1.44		$6.19
Number purchased	50		41		34		8
Total cost	$50		$49.20		$48.96		
Sales Activity							
Number sold	50		41		34		
Selling price	$2.00		$2.40		$2.88		
Income Statement							
Sales	$100		$98.40		$97.92		
Cost of sales	50		49.20		48.96		
Gross margin	50		49.20		48.96		
Expenses	45		44.20		43.96		
Net profit	5		5.00		5.00		
Begin owners equity	50		50.00		50.00		
	55		55.00		55.00		
Less dividends	5		5.00		5.00		
End owners equity	$ 50		$50.00		$50.00		

WTC's president was somewhat disturbed by the accountant's projection. Though he noted with satisfaction that the forecast showed a good steady dividend, he worried a bit about the declining number of widgets handled. It occurred to him that at some point the number might reach zero. When asked, the accountant acknowledged that in the 22nd year the company would have funds for only one widget, which by then would cost $45.96. The next year a widget would cost $55.15, exceeding the $50 cash on hand.

The president figured that a lot could happen in 23 years that might reverse the downward trend. But just in case things didn't get better, he decided to switch to a more conservative 50% dividend payout.

The accountant agreed that this change would help, but he drew up Exhibit 10-2 to show that by the 31st year WTC would be out of business.

**Exhibit 10-2
Widget Purchases
if 50% of
Profit Retained**

	Year 1	2	3	11	21	31
Cash beginning of the year starting equity plus retained earnings	$50.00	$52.50	$55.13	$81.44	$132.66	$216.10
Cost per widget	1.00	1.20	1.44	6.19	38.30	237.00
Number purchased	50	43	39	13	3	0

Then the accountant showed that even if all the profit were retained, the number of widgets that WTC could purchase would still decline, as shown in Exhibit 10-3.

**Exhibit 10-3
Widget Purchases
if all Profit
is Retained**

	Year 1	2	3	11	21	31
Cash beginning of the year	$50.00	$55.00	$60.50	$130.00	$336.00	$832.00
Cost per widget	1.00	1.20	1.44	6.19	38.30	237.00
Number purchased	50	45	42	21	8	3

On seeing this the president asked what would happen if he borrowed enough money each year to enable WTC to continue buying 50 widgets. With a little help from their banker he thought that WTC ought to be able to keep going at the 50-widget level.

To examine this proposal the accountant drew up Exhibit 10-4.[1] Since he wanted to see if the firm held a future for him, he extended his forecasts. He found that each year the amount that WTC needed to borrow increased. In year seven the required debt would just equal equity. The firm would show a profit until that year, but thereafter rising interest expense would cause it to show increasing losses. In year 10 debt would be $193.47, over three times the decreased equity of $64.53. By year 14 the equity would become negative, a

---

[1] Several assumptions about the debt were made here. The full amount of purchase price would be needed January 1 and the debt would not be repaid until December 31 each year. The interest would be 20%, the same rate as inflation.

Exhibit 10-4

WIDGET TRADING COMPANY LTD.
Pro Forma Statements with Borrowing to Stay at 50 per Year

	Year 1 Begin	Year 1 End	Year 2 Begin After Purch.	Year 2 End	Year 3 Begin After Purch.	Year 3 End	Year 4 Begin After Purch.	Year 4 End	Year 5 Begin After Purch.	Year 5 End	Year 6 Begin After Purch.	Year 6 End	Year 7 Begin After Purch.	Year 7 End
Balance Sheet														
Cash	$50	$55	0	60.0	0	64.8	0	69.12	0	72.58	0	74.66	0	74.66
Inventory	0	0	60	0	72	0	86.40	0	103.68	0	124.42	0	149.30	0
Total assets	50	55	60	60.0	72	64.8	86.40	69.12	103.68	72.58	124.42	74.66	149.30	74.66
Liabilities	0	0	5	0	12	0	21.60	0	34.56	0	51.84	0	74.64	0
Owners equity	50	55	55	55	60	64.8	64.80	69.12	69.12	72.58	72.58	74.66	74.66	74.66
Total L+OE	50	55	60	60.0	72	64.8	86.40	69.12	103.68	72.58	124.42	74.66	149.30	74.66
Cost per widget	$1.00		$1.20		$1.44		$1.73		$2.07		$2.49		$2.99	
Number purchased	50		50		50		50		50		50		50	
Total cost	$50		$60		$72		$86.40		$103.68		$124.42		$149.30	
Sales Activity														
Number sold	50		50		50		50		50		50		50	
Selling price	$2.00		$2.40		$2.88		$3.46		$4.15		$4.98		$5.97	
Income Statement														
Sales	$100		120		144		172.80		207.36		248.84		298.60	
Cost of sales	50		60		72		86.40		103.68		124.42		149.30	
Gross margin	50		60		72		86.40		103.68		124.42		149.30	
Expenses	45		54		64.8		77.76		93.31		111.97		134.37	
Interest	—		1		2.4		4.32		6.91		10.37		14.93	
Net profit	5		5		4.8		4.32		3.46		2.08		(0)	
Begin owners equity	50		55		60.0		64.8		69.12		72.58		74.66	
Total	55		60		64.8		69.12		72.58		74.66		74.66	
Less dividends	0		0		0		0		0		0		0	
End owners equity	55		60		64.8		69.12		72.58		74.66		74.66	

sad result since throughout the 14 years the owners would have received no dividends.

At this point the president realized that whether WTC retained all the profit or borrowed money or did both, the firm had a limited life span. He had thought the firm profitable, but actually it was embarked on a sure course to liquidation!

CONCLUSIONS FROM THE WTC SITUATION

It is clear that the Widget Trading Company was not making the profit shown in the income statement. In fact it was incurring a loss. To understand why WTC is incurring a loss, we have to define what we mean by *profit*.

There have been many definitions of *profit*, but the one that we believe makes the most sense is the following:

> Profit is the amount that can be paid out to the owners of the enterprise without reducing its basic capital.

This means that a firm must earn at least enough to keep going at the same level of operation before it can show a profit. Only amounts above that level of earnings can be termed *profit*. Thus, the expenses during a period are whatever it takes to allow the firm to continue during the next period at the same level of operation. For the Widget Trading Company's first year, total expense will include the $45 of current expenses plus the $60 cost of replacing the 50 widgets of basic capital. When this total of $105 is charged against WTC's revenue of $100, we see that WTC was actually incurring a loss of $5 rather than the profit of $5 shown on the income statement.

The only way that the firm could make a $5 profit in the first year would be to increase revenues by $10 or decrease expenses by $10. If WTC increased its revenues by raising its price for widgets, Exhibit 10-5 shows what would happen in year 1.

Exhibit 10-5

	As Shown for Year 1	Using Replacement Cost	New Price and Replacement Cost	New Price Historical Cost
Sales	100	100	110	110
Cost of Sales:				
Historic	50			50
Replacement	—	60	60	—
Gross Margin	50	40	50	60
Expenses	45	45	45	45
Net Profit	5	(5)	5	15
Return on Equity	10%	(10%)	10%	30%

Column 1 presents the picture the managers would normally see. The $50 cost of widgets sold is the actual dollars paid, and represents the generally accepted historical cost method of accounting. Column 2 uses the replacement cost, or what it would take to restore the firm's basic store of capital or widgets. This column shows that WTC would actually incur a loss.

If the price of widgets were raised to $2.20 each, revenue would be $110 and the firm would show a profit of $5, which could be paid out without impairing basic capital. This result is shown in Column 3. If WTC pursued this course of action, generally accepted accounting practice would still require use of historical cost accounting for external reporting and the income statement in Column 4 would result. WTC's profit would appear to be a 30% return on equity and WTC might be faced with demands for higher wages and dividends and would perhaps be charged with making monopolistic profits.

WTC's dilemma is like that of many companies. One course of action leads to slow liquidation of the business; the other results in a picture of excessive profits. There is no clear solution to this awkward situation until generally accepted measures of profit reflect the realities caused by inflation.

Several other conclusions follow from this avenue of analysis.

1. *Measuring Expenses as Replacement Costs.* If we define profit as what is left over after restoring a firm's basic capital, then the replacement cost of all assets must be considered. Inventory was WTC's only asset other than cash. Other firms have fixed assets and receivables. Replacement cost depreciation on fixed assets is the cost to replace that portion of the life of the fixed assets that is used up during the year. Receivables will also be replaced at higher dollar amounts, for if sales are increased by inflation, receivables will also have to increase if the days of receivables are to be kept constant. An increase in trade payables will offset some of this increase in assets.

Inflation requires that a higher number of dollars be invested in assets if their real value is to be maintained. These funds must come from somewhere, preferably net income. Exhibit 10-6 shows the relationship that must be maintained between capital and assets, or assets minus current liabilities which we call *net assets employed*.

Exhibit 10-6

Net Assets Employed Current Assets plus Net Fixed Assets minus Current Liabilities equals Net Assets Employed.	Net assets employed will increase each year at the rate of inflation. Conceptually this increase is like a *use of cash*.
Capital Long-term debt plus Equity equals the Capital supporting the Net Assets Employed.	Since capital must equal net assets employed; inflation will require that capital increase at least at the rate of inflation. Conceptually this increase is like a required *source of cash*.

2. *Measuring Profitability as Return on Equity.* The foregoing analysis leads to a second conclusion, that a rough rule of thumb holds that the rate of return on equity must be greater than inflation for a firm to be making any real profit. In Column 1 of Exhibit 10-5, we see that WTC's profit was $5 on $50 equity or 10%. That is less than the 20% inflation rate, and should show that WTC was really showing a loss of 10% on equity. In Column 4,

the 30% return shown is really a 10% return on equity, given the 20% inflation rate.

One can also use Exhibit 10-6 to explain this rule. The rate of increase in net assets employed equals inflation (given no real growth) so capital must also increase by the rate of inflation. If capital is all equity, the rule is clear: equity must increase by the rate of inflation, which means profit as a percent of equity must be at least equal to inflation.

The existence of long-term debt somewhat complicates this analysis but the rule still holds. Debt can be increased at the rate of inflation without increasing the real value of the liability—in the equivalent number of widgets or loaves of bread, for example. This increase represents a source of cash which can fund part of the increase in net assets employed. So equity still needs to increase, but only at the rate of inflation to cover the balance of the increase in net assets employed.

In practice this rough rule of thumb is likely to yield slightly exaggerated conclusions when applied to published financial statements. Companies which use last in first out accounting are close to using the replacement cost for inventory. This may represent a major adjustment from the first in first out historical cost method. Use of accelerated depreciation methods also tend to increase the amount of depreciation charged, though a decision to use accelerated depreciation may have little to do with inflation. Use of these two adjustments means that some companies have made part of the adjustment to replacement cost accounting and for them the threshold return on equity will not be as high as the rate of inflation.

3.   *Recognizing Asset Turnover as a Key to Inflation's Impact.* Asset turnover (sales divided by assets) will affect the impact of inflation. Industries, companies or products with low asset turnover will feel a greater impact from inflation. These are capital intensive businesses such as utilities, railroads or chemical firms. Overcoming the effects of inflation by increasing net income will be harder for these companies. Exhibit 10-7 illustrates this by showing how much three firms in different businesses would have to raise prices to provide the necessary increase in net income.

**Exhibit 10-7
Effect of
Asset Turnover
on Pricing
Inflation at 10%**

	Company A High Turnover (Assembly or Merchandising)	Company B Medium Turnover	Company C Low Turnover (Utility or Chemical Co.)
Sales Price before considering Inflation	$1.00	$1.00	$1.00
Sales	$ 100	$ 100	$ 200
Net Assets Employed (Assets Minus Trade Payables)	$ 50	$ 100	$ 200
Asset Turnover	2	1	.5
Replacement Cost of Net Assets Employed assuming 10% Inflation	$ 55	$ 110	$ 220
Sales Price Required to Cover Replacement Cost	$1.05	$1.10	$1.20

Company A needs only to raise its price 5% to cover the $5 increase in replacement cost of assets from $50 to $55. Company C, on the other hand, needs $20 more so has to raise its prices 20%. Thus, companies or product lines with low asset turnover are most vulnerable to the effects of inflation.

4.   *Recognizing Inflation's Impact on the Cost of Granting Credit.* A firm with 30 days of receivables is paying for a month's cost of the capital tied up. This cost is a well recognized part of determining appropriate credit terms. Inflation, however, adds to this cost in a way that is not so widely understood. The money received a month after sale is worth less than it would have been if received at the time of sale. If inflation is at 12%, the money loses purchasing power at the rate of 1% a month.

If a firm is considering extended terms, from 30 to 90 days, for example, the cost of the increase should be computed as follows, assuming 12% inflation, 15% cost of funds, and $1,000 of credit granted.

	30 Day Cost	90 Day Cost	Increase
Cost of Funds at 15%...............	$12.50	$37.50	$25,00
Loss of Purchasing Power at 12%.....	10.00	30.00	20.00
Total Cost........................	$22.50	$67.50	$45.00

Instead of the increase in cost of extended terms being at the rate of 1.25% per month, or $25.00 for the two month extension, we now see that the cost is really 2.25% per month or $45.00 for the new terms. Granting extended credit is much more expensive under conditions of inflation.

REQUIRED INFLATION ADJUSTMENTS IN EXTERNAL FINANCIAL REPORTS

Large, publicly held companies are now required to present certain inflation adjusted data as part of their financial reports. General Electric, whose financial statements are presented in Appendix B, included a particularly thorough and clear explanation of these adjustments. We have included them here as representative of the information now being provided to stockholders and potential investors.

One can see that reported net earnings have been reduced from about $1.5 billion to about $1 billion. Around 70% of this reduction is due to the higher replacement cost of depreciable assets, causing a higher adjusted depreciation expense, and about 30% is due to higher replacement costs of inventory. The inventory or cost of goods sold adjustment is relatively small because GE uses LIFO accounting for most of its inventories.

While these adjustments require a number of estimates in their computation, and hence are not as exact as accounting based on historical cost, they do represent a useful effort to present a more realistic picture of corporate earnings. Inflation has indeed had an effect, and while it is difficult to measure that effect precisely, it is important to recognize its existence.

GENERAL ELECTRIC ANNUAL REPORT 1980

Inflation in the U.S. continued at a high level during 1980, and most economists currently forecast double-digit rates again in 1981. Your management has stressed repeatedly the distortion that inflation has on the traditional methods of financial reporting. This distortion affects individuals, companies, and aggregate financial data on which national policy decisions are based.

The chart below highlights this distortion by comparing reported after-tax earnings with *real* after-tax earnings for all U.S. nonfinancial corporations for the years 1975 through 1980. Three inflation-related factors account for the difference between reported earnings and real earnings: underdepreciation, reflecting the shortfall from writing off facilities using acquired rather than replacement costs; "phantom" profits which occur when lower than current costs of inventory output are charged against revenues; and the loss by more than one-third in the general purchasing power of a dollar since 1975.

**Reported and Real Profits of
U.S. Nonfinancial Corporations**

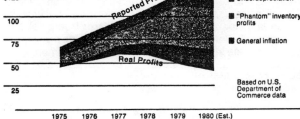

Billions
$125

100

75

50

25

■ Underdepreciation

■ "Phantom" inventory profits

■ General inflation

Based on U.S. Department of Commerce data

1975   1976   1977   1978   1979   1980 (Est.)

As reported, the aggregate after-tax earnings of all U.S. nonfinancial corporations grew each year except for a small decrease in 1980. The average annual growth rate as reported since 1975 was about 13%.

However, after adjustment for inflation, real earnings in 1980 were lower than any other year during the period, and actually have declined since 1975 at an average rate of about 2% per year.

These data indicate that corporations, just like individuals, are suffering from the pernicious effects of inflation. It is of vital importance to all Americans that intelligent and forceful action be taken to begin the long and arduous task of removing the main controllable causes of inflation — growth of the public sector at the expense of the private sector accompanied by burgeoning federal deficits and nonproductive regulation.

Your Company's financial results are not immune to the distorting effects of inflation. Financial data elsewhere in this Annual Report, including the audited financial statements, are presented using the traditional basis of financial reporting which does not fully identify the effects of inflation. The table at upper right presents information which supplements the traditional financial statements in order to gauge the effect of changing prices on results for 1980.

Supplementary Information Effect of Changing Prices	For the year ended December 31, 1980		
		Adjusted for (a)	
(In millions; except per-share amounts)	As reported	general inflation	current costs
Sales of products and services to customers	$24,959	$24,959	$24,959
Cost of goods sold	17,751	17,904	17,892
Selling, general and administrative expense	4,258	4,258	4,258
Depreciation, depletion and amortization	707	1,052	1,092
Operating costs	22,716	23,214	23,242
Operating margin	2,243	1,745	1,717
Other income	564	564	564
Interest and other financial charges	(314)	(314)	(314)
Earnings before income taxes	2,493	1,995	1,967
Provision for income taxes	(958)	(958)	(958)
Minority interest	(21)	(8)	(8)
Net earnings	$ 1,514	$ 1,029	$ 1,001
Earnings per share	$ 6.65	$ 4.52	$ 4.40
Effective tax rate	38.4%	48.0%	48.7%
Share owners' equity at Dec. 31	$ 8,200	$12,377	$12,913

(a) In dollars of average 1980 purchasing power

This table shows two different ways of attempting to remove inflationary impacts from financial results as traditionally reported. In both "adjusted for" columns, restatements are made to (1) cost of goods sold for the current cost of replacing inventories, and (2) depreciation for the current cost of plant and equipment. The column headed "general inflation" uses only a broad index to calculate the restatement, while the column headed "current costs" uses data more specifically applicable to GE.

The restatements to cost of goods sold are relatively small for GE because extensive use of last-in, first-out inventory accounting already largely reflects current costs in the traditional earnings statement. However, restatements to depreciation, which allocates plant and equipment costs to expenses over time, are relatively large because of the high rate of inflation, particularly in the last three years. This is because traditional reporting of depreciation based on original cost does not adequately reflect higher prices for replacement of productive capacity of

General Electric Annual Report 1980 Continued:

fixed assets which were purchased a number of years ago. Both of these methods of adjusting for inflation result in lower earnings than traditionally reported.

Significantly, because inflation adjustments are not allowable for tax purposes, the "real" tax rate was about 10 points higher than in traditional statements.

Your management believes the "current cost" method is more representative of GE's results, but emphasizes the considerable subjectivity involved in the calculations. These types of adjusted data are likely to be more useful in reviewing trends over a period of time, rather than in making comparisons of restatements for any one period or in specific analyses of one period compared with another. GE's after-tax earnings on the traditional basis of accounting have been higher each year from 1976 through 1980. Since 1975, a recession year like 1980, the average annual growth rate for earnings as reported was about 16%. Using the "current cost" method of removing the effects of inflation, earnings were as depicted on the green bars in the chart below. This shows a pattern similar to earnings as reported on the traditional basis, with an average annual growth rate since 1975 of about 24%.

After-Tax Earnings of General Electric Adjusted for Current Costs

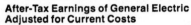

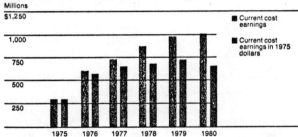

However, the purchasing power of a dollar in 1980 had diminished by more than one-third since 1975. To reflect this deterioration of the dollar's purchasing power, the blue bars in the chart express current-cost earnings for the years since 1975 in dollars of 1975 purchasing power. Even on this basis, the data indicate a real average annual growth rate in earnings since 1975 of about 14%.

General Electric's real annual growth rate of 14% in earnings since 1975 contrasts with the trend in real earnings for the aggregate of all U.S. nonfinancial corporations. As shown on page 30, aggregate earnings for all U.S. nonfinancial corporations declined during the 1975-1980 period at an average rate of about 2% per year.

Dealing with inflation as it affects your Company requires identifying the distorting effects of inflation, understanding them, recognizing them in business planning,

and managing assets and operations so as to overcome the effects of inflation.

The Company is conducting an internal program titled Effectively Coping with Inflation. This program helps participants to understand chronic high inflation, realize how it distorts financial data, and learn how to minimize the impact. More than 3,000 key managers and professionals participated in this program through 1980.

Effective asset management through differentiated capital resource allocation is especially important in coping with inflation. Investment in modern plant and equipment provides a direct effect on operations by improving productivity in the face of escalating costs. The Company's commitment to improving productivity is demonstrated by substantial increases in expenditures for new plant and equipment during recent years. In addition, strategic emphasis is placed on those business opportunities having inflation-protection characteristics. As one example, General Electric Credit Corporation owns over $5 billion of assets leased to others. Many of these assets offer significant potential gains on residual values after expiration of the leases.

Technical notes. The effect of changing prices on General Electric as set forth on page 30 has been prepared in accordance with Financial Accounting Standards Board (FASB) requirements. Information in the following table presents additional data in accordance with FASB requirements.

Current cost information in average dollars of 1980 purchasing power(a)

(In millions except per-share amounts)

	Sales	Net earnings (b)	Share owners' equity Dec. 31 (b)	Per common share Earnings (b)	Per common share Dividends	Per common share Market price Dec. 31	Purchasing power gain (loss) (c)
1980	$24,959	$1,001	$12,913	$4.40	$2.95	$59	$(198)
1979	25,493	1,119	12,659	4.93	3.12	54	(237)
1978	24,819	1,092	12,508	4.79	3.16	57	(145)
1977	23,817	1,001	12,095	4.40	2.86	66	(69)
1976	22,717	885	11,947	3.92	2.46	79	(23)
1975	21,590	479	11,414	2.13	2.45	68	22

(a) Average 1980 dollars, using the U.S. Consumer Price Index (1967 = 100): 1975–161.2; 1976–170.5; 1977–181.5; 1978–195.4; 1979–217.4; and 1980–246.8.
(b) Current cost basis.
(c) On net monetary items.

Proper use of supplementary information concerning the effect of changing prices requires an understanding of certain basic concepts and definitions.

In the table on page 30, "as reported" refers to information drawn directly from the financial statements and notes on pages 34 to 45. This information is prepared using generally accepted accounting principles which ren-

General Electric Annual Report 1980 Continued:

der an accounting based on the number of actual dollars involved in transactions, with no recognition given to the fact that the value of the dollar changes over time.

"Adjusted for general inflation" refers to information prepared using a different approach to transactions involving inventory and property, plant and equipment assets. Under this procedure, the number of dollars involved in transactions at different dates are all restated to equivalent amounts in terms of the general purchasing power of the dollar as it is measured by the Consumer Price Index for all Urban Consumers (CPI-U). For example, $1,000 invested in a building in 1967 would be restated to its 1980 dollar purchasing power equivalent of $2,468 to value the asset and calculate depreciation charges. Similarly, the 1979 purchases of non-LIFO inventory sold in 1980 would be accounted for at their equivalent in terms of 1980 dollars, rather than in terms of the actual number of dollars spent. Using this method, earnings for 1979 in 1980 dollars were $1,208 million ($5.31 per share) and share owners' equity at December 31, 1979, was $11,845 million.

"Adjusted for current costs" refers to information prepared using a third approach to inventory and property, plant and equipment transactions. In this case, rather than restating to dollars of the same general purchasing power, estimates of specific current costs of the assets are used. Principal types of information used to adjust for changes in specific prices (current costs) are: for inventory costs, GE-generated indices of price changes for specific goods and services; and for property, plant and equipment, externally generated indices of price changes for major classes of assets. Data for mineral resource assets have been adjusted by applying internally generated indices to reflect current costs. Adjustments for oil and gas properties are based on industry indices.

At December 31, 1980, the current cost of inventory was $5,701 million, and of property, plant and equipment was $8,797 million ($5,251 million and $7,004 million, respectively, at December 31, 1979). In dollars of average 1980 purchasing power, estimated current costs applicable to such assets increased during 1980, or during the part of the year the assets were held, by approximately $1,356 million, which was $196 million less than the $1,552 million increase which could be expected because of general inflation. The comparable increase for 1979 in dollars of average 1980 purchasing power was approximately $1,261 million, which was $373 million less than the $1,634 million increase which could be expected because of general inflation.

In presenting results of either of the supplementary accounting methods for more than one year, real trends are more evident when results for all years are expressed in terms of the general purchasing power of the dollar for a designated period. Results of such restatements are generally called "constant dollar" presentations. In the six-year presentations shown at left, dollar results for earlier periods have been restated to their equivalent number of constant dollars of 1980 general purchasing power (CPI-U basis).

Because none of these restatements is allowable for tax purposes under existing laws, income tax amounts are the same as in the traditional statements (but expressed in constant dollars).

All average annual growth rates in this Report use the "least squares" method of calculation.

There are a number of other terms and concepts which may be of interest in assessing the significance of the supplementary information shown. However, it is management's opinion that the basic concepts discussed above are the most significant for the reader to have in mind while reviewing this information.

Appendix A

Basic Accounting Processes Used in Preparing Financial Statements

A firm owns some things like inventory, machines and accounts receivable from customers. These are called assets. Usually a firm will also owe money to people, to suppliers, banks or bond holders. As such the firm has liabilities. If assets exceed liabilities, the difference, called "net assets," represents the owners equity in the business.

During the year many transactions take place, affecting assets, liabilities or owners' equity. We shall look at some of these in a minute, but first let us see how double-entry bookkeeping helps keep track of all these transactions.

We start with the equation reflected in the first paragraph:

Assets minus Liabilities = Owners Equity

or

Assets = Liabilities plus Owners Equity

Now try thinking of the second equation as a balance or set of scales:

The scale must always be in balance. We can exchange one asset for another (cash for raw material) and not upset the balance. Or we can reduce an asset and a liability (cash used to pay back bank debt). Profit comes about when we have a net increase in assets. For example, we might receive cash of $120 for a product with an asset value of $100. To keep in balance, owners equity must increase $20 which is the profit on the transaction.

With thousands or millions of transactions to record we need a system to translate what happens in each transaction into accounting terms which define the transaction's effect on assets, liabilities or owners equity. The system used by virtually every business, called double-entry bookkeeping, enables all transactions to be recorded in a way that keeps the books balanced. The records consist of "accounts," with names such as cash, accounts receivable, inventory, trade payables. Some of these accounts are "permanent" and their balances on December 31 make up the firm's balance sheet. Other accounts are "temporary" and disappear at the end of the year. Most of these temporary accounts are expense or revenue accounts and their

Asset accounts

Left hand (Debit) Balance or increase	Right hand (Credit) Decrease

Examples:
  Cash
  Accounts receivable
  Inventory
  Plant, equipment

Liabilities accounts

Left hand (Debit) Decrease	Right hand (Credit) Balance or increase

Examples:
  Trade payables
  Accrued wages
  Long term debt

Owners equity accounts

Left hand (Debit) Decrease	Right hand (Credit) Balance or increase

Examples:
  Capital stock
  Retained earnings

balances are transferred to a profit and loss account; this in turn is closed to the retained earnings account which is one of the owners equity accounts. Each account has a left hand and a right hand. (A left hand balance or entry is called a debit, a right hand balance or entry is called a credit, but don't worry about these labels just now.) To see how the left and right hand entries to the accounts work, we must expand our picture of the accounting equation (assets = liabilities plus owners equity) so that all the accounts have space for both left and right hand entries.

Every account has a left and a right. The balances shown in asset accounts are usually on the left, and balances in liability and owners equity accounts are usually on the right. At any one time the total of all the left hand balances must equal the total of all the right hand balances. Double-entry bookkeeping keeps this overall balance because every transaction or event is translated into both left and right hand entries and for each transaction the left entries must equal the right entries. Here are some examples:

Transaction	Left hand entry	Right hand entry
Purchase of material on account	An increase in the inventory asset account is a left hand entry	An increase in the accounts payable liability account is a right hand entry
Payment of the bill	Accounts Payable (decrease in liability account)	Cash (decrease in asset account)
Payment of employees who work on the material	Material in process (increase—asset)	Cash (decrease—asset)
Rent on office	Expense for period (decrease—owners equity)	Cash (decrease—asset)
Sale—revenue part	Accounts Receivable (increase—asset)	Sales (increase—owners equity)
Sale—cost part	Cost of goods sold (decrease—owners equity)	Finished goods (decrease—asset)

Notice that the first three of these are simply transfers among asset and liability accounts. Rent, however, decreases owner equity. Whereas the payment to production employees was "capitalized" (i.e., added to an asset) the rent was "expensed" (i.e., considered an immediate reduction in owners equity). The labor cost will also be expensed later when the inventory asset to which it is added, is sold. Until that time it is held as an asset and does not affect owners equity.

We can see that the transactions which affect owners equity are those that give rise to the income statement. In effect the income statement can be considered as a temporary subset of accounts within the owners equity set of accounts. The income statement account, or as it is sometimes called the "profit and loss account," is one of the temporary accounts. At the end of the period, when financial statements are to be prepared, the balance remaining in the profit and loss account is the difference between all the expenses (debits to the P&L account) and revenues (credits to the P&L account). This is the net profit for the period and at this point it is transferred to the retained earnings account. This "closes" the P&L account to zero so it can start from scratch in the next period. The P&L account is a "temporary" account and as such does not show up among the permanent balance sheet accounts. The retained earnings account is permanent. It is increased by net profit after tax and decreased by payment of dividends.

DEBITS AND CREDITS

The terms debit and credit in accounting mean nothing more or less than left hand entry (debit) and right hand entry (credit). A debit entry may be an increase in an asset or a decrease in a liability or owners equity account. A credit is just the opposite. The word credit sometimes carries a favorable connotation, but as one can see, a credit, such as a decrease in cash or an increase in notes payable, is not necessarily good. The term probably gets its favorable connotation by being looked at by an outsider, a customer for example. When a customer gets credit from a store for overpayment of a bill or returned merchandise, this increases the store's liability to the customer (or decreases its receivables). This is good for the customer but bad for the store. So remember: debit = left hand entry; credit = right hand entry.

COST ACCUMULATION

When costs are incurred to run a business and to produce a product, the accountant must decide whether the costs are to be capitalized (e.g., added to inventory) or expensed right away. In making this decision the accountant has some leeway, but basically the determination rests on whether they are factory costs, sometimes called costs under the factory roof. Factory costs, whether labor, material or overhead, are added to the inventory cost of the product. This determination can affect profits because any costs which are added to inventory which in turn is not sold during the period, are not expenses of that period. And, incidentally, this shows the difference between costs and expenses. A cost is an expense only if it becomes a debit (decrease) in owners equity and hence shows up on the income statement. Costs which are added to unsold inventory are not expenses of the period. They become expenses when the inventory is sold, and appear as cost of goods sold on the income statement for that period.

BALANCE SHEET AND INCOME STATEMENTS

The balance sheet presents a picture at a point in time of the balances in the asset, liability and owners equity accounts. The income statement shows the change in the retained earnings account from one balance sheet date to the next. (The other accounts under owners equity, such as capital stock, capital in excess of par value, preferred stock, do not generally change unless shares of stock are sold or a stock dividend is declared.) The income statement, therefore, tells how much profit the firm made which is the same as saying how much the owners equity increased during the period as a result of operations.

By comparing two balance sheets, e.g., last year's and this year's, we can tell how the composition of assets and liabilities changed during the intervening period. This is important because it reflects such things as liquidity, debt position, etc. If assets shift from short-term receivables into long-term fixed assets, the firm's liquidity or ability to come up with cash quickly, is diminished. If this happens while short-term debt is being increased, a dangerous condition could result from using short-term money to buy long-term assets.

Ratios are helpful in analyzing balance sheets, ratios such as the "current ratio" which is current assets (cash, receivables and inventory) divided by current liabilities (payables due within a year) and debt to equity ratio. Often the absolute level of a ratio is less important than its trend or speed of change. A high debt-equity ratio may be good or bad depending on the type of business. However, a rapidly increasing debt equity ratio is almost always cause for concern and may be very difficult to reverse. Appendix B has further discussion of the use of ratios in analyzing financial statements.

CASH FLOW VERSUS NET INCOME

One might expect that the excess of revenue over expenses (which is net income) would result in an increase in the cash account by the same amount. This almost never happens because there are many factors which would cause this not to be true. They fall into two basic categories:

a. Some expenses recorded in the income statement may not represent cash expenditure during the period (e.g., depreciation) and some revenue may not represent cash inflow (e.g., amortization of customer advance payments).

b. Increases or decreases in assets, liabilities and owners equity accounts (the latter for reasons other than net income) will imply a source or application of cash. For example, if inventory rises from January 1 to December 31, this implies an application or use of cash in that the firm has apparently spent cash in buying inventory. Of course if payables to suppliers went up at the same time, this would represent a source of cash, a source because in effect the firm is borrowing cash from the suppliers. From this we can see the following:

Uses of cash come about with increases in assets, decreases in liabilities or decreases in owners equity.

Sources of cash come about with decreases in assets, increases in liabilities or increases in owners equity.

Recently companies have been publishing a statement (along with their annual balance sheet and income statement) called "Statement of Changes in Financial Position." This statement is a listing of sources and uses of funds for the year. The term "funds" is most often taken as working capital (current assets minus current liabilities) but an increasing number of firms are dropping that formulation and taking funds to mean cash. Appendix B explains this statement further and shows how it can be usefully analyzed.

Appendix B

Understanding Financial Statements

The financial reports which are issued quarterly and annually by companies contain a wealth of information for those who know how to extract it. The purpose of this appendix is to help you discover what these reports can tell you. The first part explains the numbers contained in the reports and the second part shows how a little analysis using ratios can reveal a lot about what is going on in the company. In this appendix, we have tried to select the most important aspects of the reports. There are many other fine points in financial accounting which only a large book could properly explore. Furthermore, since the financial accounting standards which guide the preparation of reports are continually being reviewed and are revised from time to time, a complete understanding of the accounting process that lies behind financial statements is a major undertaking. Our purpose here is to explain the basic items you will find in most statements and, without attempting to exhaust all possibilities, to show how a little analysis can greatly increase the amount you can learn from these reports.

THE THREE BASIC FINANCIAL STATEMENTS

Published annual reports are now required to contain these three statements:

The *Balance Sheet* or Statement of Financial Position. This shows the firm's assets, liabilities, and owners equity, usually both for last year and for this year.

The *Income Statement* or Statement of Earnings shows revenues, expenses, and net income for the period. A few lines may be added to this statement showing how retained earnings changed during the year. The information is included at the end of the income statement because often the only items which change retained earnings are net income from the income statement and dividends. When there are more changes in retained earnings, a longer statement will show the beginning and ending retained earnings balances which clearly tie in with the balance sheets.

The *Statement of Changes in Financial Position* explains where funds came from during the year, such as from net income or from borrowing, and where funds went or what they were used for, such as for capital expenditures and debt repayment. The net of these sources and applications is the year's increase or decrease in "funds." Most companies define "funds" as their working capital (current assets minus current liabilities). With this approach, the concept of funds is one of short-term liquidity. The Statement of Changes in Financial Position will then have three parts:

1. Source of Funds

2. Application of Funds
    Net Change in Funds or Working Capital

3. Changes in the Elements of Working Capital
    Net Change in Working Capital

The third part will show what changes in cash, receivables, inventory, and payables caused the change in working capital, which is also the net figure from the sources and applications of funds.

Some companies go further and define funds to be cash rather than working capital. In these instances, the statement will have only two parts, the year's sources of cash and the year's use or application of cash, all balancing out to the net change in cash. The General Electric Company follows this second approach.

EXPLANATION OF THE BALANCE SHEETS

This discussion will follow the entries shown in the General Electric Company's statements, copies of which are at the end of this appendix. These serve us well because they have been condensed to a relatively small number of entries and are clearly stated.

First, notice the overall balance sheet structure.

Current Assets	Current Liabilities
Non-Current Assets	Non-Current Liabilities
Total Assets	Total Liabilities
	Preferred Stock
	Common Stock
	Retained Earnings
	Total Owners Equity
	Total Liabilities and Equity

General Electric puts all of this on one page so they are lined up vertically. However, one can see that the double underlined figures are the same so the balance sheet balances.

One can also see that the balance sheet follows the accounting format which was explained in Appendix A in which the assets have the left hand balances and the liabilities and owners equity accounts have right hand balances.

Items are separated into current and non-current categories to help analysts see the balance between current assets and current liabilities. Working capital is the amount by which current assets exceed current liabilities. In a way, working capital says how much cash the firm would have if it turned all its current assets into cash and paid off current liabilities. But, since few firms are about to do that, the liquidation view is rather artificial. However, creditors who are lending to a company do view working capital as sort of a liquidity cushion, or as a funds reservoir needed to keep the enterprise operating smoothly. Since some kinds of businesses naturally need more operating funds than others, creditors are concerned less with the level of that reservoir than with how the level changes from period to period. A sizable decrease could impair the firm's ability to operate.

A "consolidated" financial statement, such as General Electric presents, means that the statements of subsidiaries (or affiliates as GE calls them) have been combined with the parent company's statements to present a consolidated picture. The process of combining is basically one of adding assets and liabilities of subsidiaries to assets and liabilities of the parent, eliminating debts (for the balance sheet) or transactions (for the income statement) between them. Subsidiaries that are more than 50% owned are usually consolidated, the exception being those subsidiaries like finance or real estate companies whose business and financial structure are completely different from those of the parent company. When a minority interest exists in a consolidated subsidiary, the consolidation process still combines 100% of the assets and liabilities but then represents the minority interest in the equity section of the balance sheet. The amount shown is based on the book value of the subsidiary's equity and the percentage of ownership.

BALANCE SHEET ITEMS

Cash. The amount shown here represents both what is in checking accounts and the ownership of short-term obligations of others such as time deposits, certificates of deposit or commercial paper. As of December 31, 1980, these totaled $1,601 million for GE.

Marketable Securities. These are likely to be interest bearing debt, of a longer term than would appear under cash. One can see that GE tends to have more cash or near cash liquidity than it would seem to need for current operations. There are a number of reasons why GE might wish to have a cushion of cash or short-term securities. At any particular time GE might be "saving up" for heavy expenditures and trying to avoid having to borrow money on short notice. Or the liquidity cushion might be there because repayment of debt, or repurchase of stock were not deemed to be appropriate uses for the cash at that time.

Current Receivables. These are amounts owed by others, usually customers. One can get a rough indication of how many days sales they represent from this formula

$$\frac{\text{Trade Receivables}}{\text{Net Sales for the Year}} \times 365 = \text{Days of Receivables}$$

For GE this is $\dfrac{4,339}{24,959} \times 365 = .174 \times 365 = 64$ days

This says that on the average, GE's receivables are outstanding 64 days before they are paid. Some, of course, are paid earlier and others later. This calculation also builds in the assumption that sales during the last quarter (which caused the receivables) were about average for the year, since the total year's sales figure was used.

If we use the fourth quarter's sales of $6,918 million, then the calculation would be more precise and look like this:

$$\begin{array}{ll} \text{Receivables:} & \dfrac{4,339}{6,918} = .63 \times 92 = 58 \text{ days} \\ \text{4th Quarter Sales:} & \end{array}$$

Inventories. The cost of raw materials, work-in-process, and finished goods are represented here. GE uses LIFO (last in, first out) for most of its inventories so the unit costs charged against income each year are based on the latest prices. This means that the costs remaining in inventory are based on old prices, some going back ten or more years to the year GE started using LIFO. GE tells us elsewhere that whereas inventory at old prices is shown at $3.3 billion, the same inventory would be about $5.6 billion at current prices.

Investments. The amount appearing here represents the firm's investment in other companies, which may be non-consolidated subsidiaries, like a finance company or companies in which there is a minority holding.

Plant, Property and Equipment. This represents all capital assets, i.e., those lasting over a year. Except for land, these assets will be depreciated each year. An amount representing the year's depreciation will be subtracted from the asset on the balance sheet and from revenue on the income statement. The income statement deduction will reduce net income, and in turn reduce the retained earnings entry on the balance sheet, thereby offsetting the decrease in fixed assets and keeping the balance sheet in balance. The $5.8 billion shown by GE on its balance sheet represents the net figure. Elsewhere GE tells us that the gross (cost) figure is $11 billion and the offsetting accumulated depreciation is $5.2 billion. On the average GE's depreciable assets are almost 50% depreciated.

Other Assets. These include a variety of items such as long-term receivables, advances to customers and prepaid expenses and taxes.

Short-Term Borrowings. These borrowings, due within a year, are from banks or other companies. One may wonder why a company like GE would have both short-term receivables under cash and short-term borrowings. The answer is partly that they are in different markets or countries and cannot be easily offset, and partly that the lending and borrowing contracts are for different numbers of days, so that on December 31 it would be impractical and expensive to recall the advances and repay the borrowings.

Accounts Payable. These are amounts owed to suppliers. For a wholesale or retail merchandising company these accounts payable represent a significant source of funds with which to run the business.

Progress Collections and Price Adjustments Accrued. GE asks customers to make partial payments on long-term contracts as the work progresses. This helps GE finance the build-up of work-in-progress. When such payments are received, GE increases cash and makes a corresponding increase in the progress collections liability. Since GE does not recognize a sale in its accounts until the job is completed (known as the "completed contract method"), it recognizes no profit on a job in its accounts until the job is finished. The alternative method, known as the "percentage of completion" method recognizes sales revenue and profit as the work progresses.

Dividends Payable. Between the date the board of directors declares a dividend and the date it is actually paid, the amount to be paid is shown as a liability of the company.

Taxes Accrued. In the case of income taxes, which are likely to be the bulk of this figure, a company accrues taxes as it earns taxable income. Periodic payments will reduce this accrued amount. At the end of a year the accrued amount is really an estimate because the financial report will probably be prepared before the firm's tax return is filed.

Other Costs and Expenses Accrued. These are a variety of smaller amounts which will be paid within a year. The largest single item for GE is accrued compensation, which includes the days of earnings which employees have earned but for which they have not yet been paid.

Long-Term Borrowings. This may be made up of several long-term bond issues, some maturing in a few years, others extending way out into the future. GE's longest term bond matures in 2004.

Other Liabilities. This includes a number of complex long-term liabilities such as deferred compensation and deferred investment tax credit.

Preferred Stock. Preferred stock is considered part of the owners equity section because there is no maturity date when the owners of the stock can expect to get their investment back. On the other hand, it has a preferred position because both in liquidation and in payment of dividends it comes before the common stock. For this preferred treatment, however, the owners give up participation in growth since the dividend is fixed and any call is at or close to par value.

Common Stock, Amounts Received in Excess of Par Value and Retained Earnings. The total of these three accounts after deducting any treasury stock represents the book value of the common stock. This can be viewed in two ways. First, it is the net assets of the corporation or in other words the amount left over when total liabilities and any preferred stock outstanding are subtracted from total assets. This is the residual value on which common stockholders have a claim. Secondly, the three accounts can be viewed separately. The common stock account represents par value of the stock outstanding. The "excess" account, sometimes called capital surplus, represents the amount the company received in excess of par value when it sold or exchanged the stock. The retained earnings account accumulates earnings that are not paid out in dividends. Basically, these three common equity accounts arise through sale of stock and through retention of earnings. However, there are other, sometimes complex, transactions that can affect the accounts, such as those that accompany mergers, stock splits and stock dividends.

Common stock held in treasury or treasury stock is stock which the company has bought in the open market. It is shown at cost. The stock is usually acquired for use in stock option plans or for use in acquisitions when the directors do not which to issue new stock.

EXPLANATION OF THE INCOME STATEMENT

The income statement presents the revenue and expenses which have taken place during the year, quarter or whatever accounting period is covered. The difference between the revenue and expense is net income.

This explanation sounds very simple, but there are many issues and decisions which lie behind the determination of revenue and expense. Here are a few:

Expense vs. Capitalized Cost

A firm spends $1 million fixing up its steam generating plant which has been operating for 10 years with only minor repairs. Is this to be considered a major repair, and therefore an expense, or an overhaul extending the generating plant's life, and therefore a capital expenditure which adds to the value of the asset and does not affect expense except through depreciation of the asset? The answer will have an effect on net income during the year of expenditure. Similar questions apply to development costs on major new product lines, as with a commercial airplane, or the costs of entering a new market such as in a foreign country.

The Timing Question

The most pervasive timing question concerns the depreciation charge. Since depreciation is a means of allocating an asset's cost over its life, the total amount of depreciation for that asset's life is fixed. Only the timing is in question. There is first the question of period, or number of years over which the asset should be depreciated; then having settled the depreciable life there is the question of pattern. Should a straight-line (the same each year) or accelerated pattern (more in the early years) be used. The choice is frequently determined more by the tax impact than by engineering evidence, but in any case the choice is one of timing and significantly affects net income. GE uses an accelerated method (sum-of-the-years' digits) for most of its depreciable assets, for both tax reporting and its financial report.

The timing question is also involved when a contract extends over several years. The question is when to recognize expense, revenue and profit. As stated earlier, GE recognizes a contract's expense, revenue and profit when the contract is completed. The "percentage of completion" method of contract accounting recognizes a portion of these in each accounting period. The latter method recognizes profit earlier and bases this profit on an estimated percent complete and an estimated amount of profit on the contract when it is completed. Use of one or the other method can make a big difference in the amount of profit reported in any particular year.

The Use of Reserves for Future Expenses or Losses

When a product is guaranteed there is likely to be warranty expense for subsequent repair of some of the products. At the time of sale, one can only guess at the amount. This guess, which creates a reserve, reduces revenue in the year of the sale. When claims come in later they are not an expense of that period, but are charged to the reserve as long as it lasts. When these charges are more or less than the reserve, the original guess is proved wrong.

Company experience helps to predict the pattern of warranty expenses so the amount of reserve needed may not be a major uncertainty. However, other potential losses can be large and unrelated to past experience, such as with the insolvency of a major customer or the expropriation of foreign assets. The probability of some loss can often be anticipated by a year or more and in such cases a reserve is customarily set up. The amount of that reserve is difficult to determine when there is no prior experience to use as a guide.

The Income Statement Format

The income statement starts with revenue and then usually subtracts first those expenses which are most closely related to operations. A manufacturing firm often separates those costs which go into inventory and goods sold from those which are administrative, selling and other ongoing expenses. The following format can then be used:

Sales Revenue
  Minus Cost of Goods Sold

Equals Gross Margin
  Minus Selling and General Administrative Expenses

Equals Operating Income
  Minus Other Expenses and Plus Other Income

Equals Net Income Before Tax
  Minus Income Tax Accrued

Equals Net Income After Tax

With this format the gross margin in total or as a percent of sales revenue can be watched. A change in the gross margin percent can be caused by two factors: a price change of a change in the cost per unit. The implications of each of these causes are, of course, very different. If gross margin percentage narrows because of erosion of selling prices, and management incorrectly thinks it is caused instead by unit cost increases, management's corrective action would lead to unpleasant consequences. It is important, therefore, to keep accounting records in such a way that changes in average price and average cost can be separately computed.

The other categories used in the income statement format are also helpful in analyzing the data. Operating income is that income which results from the operation of the main business. Operating income is then separated from other income and expenses which may be from financial transactions or unusual circumstances that are expected to vary greatly from year to year. These separations in the format will then help the reader analyze the different parts of the firm's activities.

General Electric does not show a cost of goods sold and consequently shows no gross margin. However, even if GE did show a gross margin, it could not be analyzed very precisely because each of the many different kinds of businesses GE is in would probably have a different gross margin percentage and the overall margin would therefore be affected by changes in the mix of business volumes as well as the actual margins.

EXPLANATION OF THE STATEMENT OF CHANGES IN FINANCIAL POSITION

This statement, which has only recently become a standard part of the annual financial report is one of the more difficult to understand fully. Yet it does provide much useful information. It describes the elements of funds flow, stating first the sources of funds and then the ways in which those funds were used. If "funds" means working capital, as is often the case, then a third section of the statement shows how the various elements of working capital changed. If "funds" means cash, as in GE's statement, then the statement will have only two parts.

Source of Funds From Operations

The statement almost always starts with net income after taxes, which is then followed by a number of items which were included in the computation of net income but which did not involve funds or cash during the year. Depreciation, usually the largest of these items, is an expense of the year and therefore reduces net income. However, it does not reflect a payment of cash this year so it is added back to net income. In the same way the minority share in profits is subtracted on the income statement, but does not constitute cash outflow. It too is added back. Items that are subtracted at this point, such as "earnings retained by non-consolidated finance affiliates" were recognized as revenue but were not cash inflows or were cash outflows but not expenses. After all these adjustments are made, cash income is almost always greater than the net income shown in the income statement.

Other Sources of Funds

These are fairly self-explanatory and may be summarized as decreases in assets or increases in liabilities or owners equity. In GE's two-part statement which includes elements of working capital in the sources and applications listings, we can see that an increase in current payables is a source of funds (cash) and an increase in long-term borrowings and common stock are also sources of funds.

Application of Funds

The two largest items here are usually capital expenditures (additions to property, plant and equipment) and dividends. Also included in this list are other increases in assets, such as receivables and decreases in liabilities, such as repayment of debt.

Changes in the Components of Working Capital

When the statement of changes in financial position is presented in three parts, and hence "funds" means working capital, the first two parts list sources and uses of working capital. The third part will show how the various working capital components changed and how those changes netted out to the change in working capital itself. This section is sometimes hard to follow, but these rules may be a helpful guide:

Working Capital is increased by:	An increase in cash, receivables or inventory. A decrease in payables and short-term debt.
Working Capital is decreased by:	A decrease in cash, receivables or inventory. An increase in payables or short-term debt.

Analyzing the Statement of Changes in Financial Position

In analyzing this statement it may help to classify the kinds of changes shown on this statement as follows using cash rather than working capital as the meaning of funds.[1]

a. Sources of cash from operations. This will be primarily net income plus depreciation.

b. Sources or applications of cash relating to working capital and including tax liability. These would include the effects of increases or decreases in receivables, inventory, trade payables and income tax accrued but exclude short-term borrowings.

These first two classifications include those sources and applications of cash which are affected by the level, method and profitability of operations. As the level of operations rises, cash will probably have to be applied to receivables and inventory though an increase in trade payables may offset this somewhat. Credit terms and inventory control methods will affect cash required to support receivables and inventory. Profitability will affect both net income from operations and tax accrued. An increase in profitability will provide a greater source in both, and a decrease in profitability will shrink the net income source and at the same time require an application of cash to reduce the amount of tax accrued. The firm gets double benefit in good times but double penalty in hard times.

c. The third category of funds (cash) flow includes application of funds for two purposes, both of which are discretionary and not directly tied to operations. These are capital expenditures and dividends. Together they usually represent a major use of cash.

d. All the other sources and applications of funds. Usually this category will include changes in short and long-term debt, sale of stock and other miscellaneous flows relating to financing and investments.

By grouping the funds flows in this manner according to type and cause, it is possible to obtain a clearer picture of a company's need for funds and how they are being provided. For example, GE's 1979 and 1980 statements can be summarized as follows:

---

[1] This discussion is based on the Coleman Cash Flow Statement designed by Professor Almand R. Coleman of the Colgate Darden Graduate School of Business Administration, University of Virginia.

General Electric: Coleman Cash Flow
(in millions of dollars)
(Application of cash is shown in parentheses)

For Years Ending December 31	1980	1979
Cash income from operations	2,339	2,053
Changes in working capital related to operations		
Increase in receivables	(692)	(358)
Increase in inventories	(182)	(158)
Increase in current payables	498	786
Net change	(376)	270
Cash from operations	1,963	2,323
Capital expenditures	(1,948)	(1,262)
Dividends	(670)	(624)
Net before other flows	(655)	437
Other sources and applications	280	(324)
Net increase (decrease) in cash and marketable securities	(375)	113

ANALYZING FINANCIAL STATEMENTS USING RATIOS AND OTHER TECHNIQUES

The generally accepted purpose of financial statements is to convey financial information of interest and importance to a firm's stockholders and potential investors. With a little mathematical analysis of these statements we can learn quite a bit about what is going on in the company.

There are, of course, some basic things the numbers tell us, such as how big the firm is, whether it was profitable, and whether assets exceed debts. (If they do not, the firm is technically bankrupt.) In addition a little analysis of ratios will produce more information which may not be immediately apparent.

There are three general types of ratios which can be computed:

— Ratios of liquidity and financial position
— Ratios of performance
— Ratios reflecting general strategy such as management's dividend and capital expenditure decisions.

We will take these up in turn and give some illustrations of each.

RATIOS OF LIQUIDITY AND FINANCIAL POSITION

To illustrate the ratios discussed here, we have computed each ratio for General Electric Company for 1980. Numbers, except per share figures, are in millions of dollars. The most frequently used ratio of liquidity is the current ratio which is

$$\text{Current Ratio} = \frac{\text{Current Assets}}{\text{Current Liabilties}} \quad \text{or} \quad \frac{9,883}{7,592} = 1.30$$

Current assets and liabilities are those assets and liabilities that are likely to be turned into cash within a year. (Cash, receivables, inventory, payables and short-term debt.) A ratio of more than one says that the firm has more than enough short-term assets to cover its short-term liabilities. A ratio of less than one may indicate financial weakness, though there are circumstances in which this is not so. A service firm (utility, communications company, leasing company) which has little or no inventory may show a current ratio of less than one while it is in normally robust financial health. Thus, one can only derive a rough indication from the level of the current ratio, and this should be taken in the context of the type of business. An average current ratio for firms in similar businesses would help show what a normal current ratio should be for the company being analyzed.

The trend of change in a current ratio over time is usually more significant than its level. A decrease in the current ratio is most often a reflection of the firm's having used short-term borrowing from suppliers or a bank either to cover losses or to buy plant and equipment. Neither of those strategies can continue indefinitely. To some extent the decrease in GE's current ratio from 1.37 in 1979 to 1.30 in 1980 reflected the latter strategy. However, with GE's level of profitability and low level of long-term debt this change should not represent a problem for GE.

A commonly used ratio of financial position is the debt ratio which shows the extent to which a company is using debt capital to finance the business. This could be shown as the ratio of debt to equity or of debt to capital, capital being equity plus long-term debt. The latter is probably the more frequently used so.

$$\text{Debt Ratio} = \frac{\text{Long-Term Debt}}{\text{Capital}} \text{ or } \frac{2,565}{10,765} = .24$$
$$(\text{Long-Term Debt} + \text{Equity})$$

The higher this ratio, the greater is the reliance on debt as a source of capital. It is also true that the higher the ratio the greater the risk, since debt involves fixed obligations of interest and principal repayment. With this risk comes higher "leverage," which may be good or bad for the equity holder. When things go well and net income rises, the equity holders get all the benefits since interest is fixed. This effect of leverage explains how some small investors have become wealthy in highly leveraged real estate ventures. On the other hand leverage is a two edged sword and there are other highly leveraged investors who have been wiped out by a relatively small decline in values and income. Among publicly held companies one is likely to see high debt leverage in public utilities, financial companies and companies with fixed salable assets like real estate. Those companies which show low debt leverage may be those which are subject to wide cyclical swings and high risk or those which have succeeded in paying down their debt and have not yet generated a need for further long-term investment.

RATIOS OF PERFORMANCE

There are many possible ratios of performance. Here are six of the most widely used performance ratios which shed light on how a firm is doing.

$$\text{Profit Margin} = \frac{\text{Net Income}}{\text{Sales}} \text{ or } \frac{1,514}{24,959} = 6.1\%$$

This tells what a company's profit is in relation to sales revenue. In some industries like food retailing or construction it is likely to be a low percentage while in others such as airlines, utilities or high technology firms it it is likely to be a higher percentage.

$$\text{Asset Turnover} = \frac{\text{Sales}}{\text{Total Assets}} \quad \text{or} \quad \frac{24{,}959}{18{,}511} = 1.35$$

If one can accept that all assets turn over in the same way that inventory turns over, this ratio tells the annual turnover of the firm's total assets. One could also say that it tells how many dollars of sales are generated by a dollar of assets.

As one would expect capital intensive businesses such as utilities, airlines and oil production and transport firms are likely to have low turnover rates. Merchandising, research and financial firms are likely to have high assets turnover. One can also see that firms with low turnover are likely to have high profit margins and vice versa.

$$\text{Return on Assets} = \frac{\text{Net Income}}{\text{Total Assets}} \quad \text{or} \quad \frac{1{,}514}{18{,}511} = 8.2\%$$

This ratio reflects closely the financial objectives of a firm. It tells how well the money invested in a firm's assets are generating profit.

The first two performance ratios can be combined to produce this third ratio as follows:

$$\text{Profit Margin } \frac{\text{Net Income}}{\text{Sales}} \times \text{Asset Turnover} \frac{\text{Sales}}{\text{Assets}} = \text{Return on Assets } \frac{\text{Net Income}}{\text{Assets}}$$

$$\text{or } 6.1\% \qquad\qquad \times 1.35 \qquad\qquad = 8.2\%$$

This is an important relationship because it shows that there are two ways in which to improve the rate of return on assets: one is to increase the profit margin and the other is to increase the asset turnover. While the former is quite obvious, the latter is less commonly recognized but equally powerful in its effect.

$$\text{Return on Equity} = \frac{\text{Net Income}}{\text{Stockholders Equity}} \quad \text{or} \quad \frac{1{,}514}{8{,}200} = 18.5\%$$

This ratio is similar to the return on assets ratio in that it measures how well the invested funds are performing. However, this ratio focuses on that part of total capital which corresponds to stockholders' ownership. The ratio will generally be higher than return on assets, and the amount by which it is higher will depend on the amount of leverage used, or strictly speaking, the relationship between stockholders equity and the total of equity plus all liabilities. The return on assets ratio shows the overall rate of return while return on equity shows what that return is when modified by the effect of financial leverage.

$$\text{Price Earnings Ratio} = \frac{\text{Market Price Per Share}}{\text{Earnings Per Share}} \quad \text{or} \quad \frac{66}{6.65} = 9.9$$

This ratio uses the price which investors are willing to pay for the company's stock, a price which will reflect their views on the company's current performance and future prospects. By relating this to earnings per share, we can see how much investors are paying for a dollar of current earnings. A P/E ratio of 5 and 6 is fairly low and probably means that investors believe the current earnings are not likely to grow very much. A P/E ratio of 12-20 probably means investors expect earnings (and consequently share price) to grow. They are willing to pay a high price for current earnings. (A high P/E ratio may also be caused by a decrease in earnings which investors expect to be temporary.)

$$\frac{\text{Earnings Per Share}}{\text{Growth Rate}} = \frac{\text{EPS Increase}}{\text{EPS Last Year}} \quad \text{or} \quad \frac{.45}{6.20} = 7.3\%$$

Since the P/E ratio is likely to be influenced by the rate of earnings growth, this ratio computes that directly. It really ought to be computed for each year for several years to discover the compound growth rate over a period of time.

In evaluating this, one should remember that any rate which is less than the prevailing inflation rate, is really no growth at all. Likewise, unless share prices increase at least with the rate of inflation, they too will not reflect any growth in real terms.

RATIOS FOR DIVIDENDS AND CAPITAL EXPENDITURE

$$\text{Dividend Payout Ratio} = \frac{\text{Dividends Paid Per Share}}{\text{Earnings Per Share for the Period}} \quad \text{or} \quad \frac{2.95}{6.65} = 44\%$$

When companies pay dividends to their common stockholders, they usually pay out only a portion of the net income. Since the amount of dividend is at the discretion of the firm's board of directors, it is not fixed by contract and may reflect longer run strategy. A payout-ratio of under 25% usually means a firm is conserving cash, either for growth or to cover maturing debts. A payout ratio above 60% usually means the company is providing a return to stockholders more in terms of dividend income than in terms of growth and share price appreciation. To test this from a different viewpoint one can relate dividend to share price to get percentage yield. If this is close to available interest rate yields on corporate bonds, the stock is probably selling on an income yield basis rather than on the basis of expected growth. GE's dividend yield was around 5% in early 1981, too low to reflect an acceptable income yield. Thus, investors in GE expected growth in dividend and share price.

In the area of capital expenditure there are two ratios which give an indication of a firm's growth rate and financial needs.

$$\text{Fixed Asset Increase Rate} = \frac{\text{Capital Expenditure}}{\begin{array}{c}\text{Fixed Assets at Cost}\\\text{Beginning of Year}\end{array}} \quad \text{or} \quad \frac{1,948}{9,365} = 21\%$$

This ratio gives some indication of the rate of renewal or increase in fixed assets. Some of that capital expenditure may be for replacement and some for increase in capacity. It is hard to tell what the split may be because the amount required for replacement depends on how long the assets last before replacement (or in other words the portion that must be replaced each year) and the rate of inflation. For example, it will cost $2.16 million to replace an asset which cost $1.0 million ten years before, if inflation has been about 8% a year.

Another approach to this same question is to relate capital expenditure to depreciation:

$$\begin{array}{c}\text{Capital Expenditure to}\\\text{Depreciation Ratio}\end{array} = \frac{\text{Capital Expenditure}}{\text{Annual Depreciation}} \quad \text{or} \quad \frac{1,948}{707} = 2.76$$

One would expect to find a ratio greater than 1.0. Even if the company were standing still, inflation would mean a higher annual replacement cost than depreciation based on the asset costs which existed in previous years. If inflation averaged 8%, and asset lives average 10 years (average age of assets owned about 5 years) then capital expenditure would be somewhere near 1.5 times depreciation.

A third ratio relates depreciation and fixed assets at cost:

$$\frac{\text{Depreciation}}{\text{Fixed Assets at Cost}} \quad \text{or} \quad \frac{707}{9,365} = 7.5\%$$

Putting these three ratios together, we can come to some rough conclusions on how much real growth the capital expenditure is supporting, and on the size of a firm's financial needs.

To estimate how much real capital expenditures have grown, we can start with the third ratio which gives an indication of the average life of property plant and equipment. If straight-line depreciation were used (the same amount per year for each asset), then it would appear that the average life is 100 ÷ the ratio percentage. For GE this would be 13.3 years. This estimate is probably understated since GE uses accelerated depreciation. With accelerated depreciation young assets acquired at inflated prices have more depreciation than if the straight-line method were used.

If we assume an average life of 15 years then in the absence of growth and inflation the ratio of capital expenditure to cost would be 6.6% (15/100). The difference between the computed 6.6% and the actual 21% is caused by inflation and real growth in capital expenditures. Given the age and inflation rates over the past 15 years, one can estimate that GE substantially increased capital expenditures in real terms in 1980.

This analysis can be extended using the capital expenditure to depreciation ratio of 2.76. If the *average* age of assets is around 7 1/2 years, then if inflation has averaged 8% over the past 15 years, the replacement cost would be about 1.65 times annual depreciation, if annual depreciation were on straight-line. Since GE uses accelerated depreciation, the expected ratio would be somewhat lower. GE's ratio of 2.76 in 1981, therefore, presents a picture in which about 60% (1.65/2.76) of the capital expenditure would be needed for replacement at higher cost, and the remaining 40% would be real growth.[2]

These ratios also provide information on the firm's need for funds. The capital expenditure to depreciation ratio (GE's was 2.76) indicates the extent to which capital expenditures exceed the depreciation allowance and require funding from other sources such as from retained earnings or borrowing. In GE's case capital expenditures of 1,948 exceeded the depreciation allowance of 707 by 1,241. Retained earnings after dividends was 844 so about 400 had to come from other sources, mainly borrowing.

THE IMPORTANCE OF TRENDS IN ANALYZING RATIOS

For most of these ratios their change over time is as revealing as their absolute level. As noted earlier, the current ratio is a good example of this. Lenders become more worried about a company which shows a declining high current ratio than about one which shows a steady but low ratio. Likewise a rising debt ratio may reveal more financial risk than one which is high but steady. The absolute level of these ratios may be conditioned by the type of business involved whereas the trends result more from what is going on in the particular company.

CONCLUSION

This discussion of ratios has covered some of the more commonly used indicators of position and performance. As you become familiar with financial statements, it is likely that others will appear useful. Each financial analyst will probably have his or her own set of ratios which he or she finds more revealing. Therefore, this discussion is more of a starting point than a comprehensive coverage of the subject.

---

[2] In its Annual Report, GE estimates depreciation based on current cost of fixed assets. This current cost depreciation is about 54% higher than the historical cost depreciation, and is 56% of actual capital expenditures. This would indicate that 44% of capital expenditures would represent real growth.

Statement of earnings

General Electric Company and consolidated affiliates

For the years ended December 31 (In millions)		1980	1979	1978
Sales	Sales of products and services to customers (note 1)	$24,959	$22,461	$19,654
Operating costs	Cost of goods sold	17,751	15,991	13,915
	Selling, general and administrative expense	4,258	3,716	3,205
	Depreciation, depletion and amortization	707	624	576
	Operating costs (notes 2 and 3)	22,716	20,331	17,696
	Operating margin	2,243	2,130	1,958
	Other income (note 4)	564	519	419
	Interest and other financial charges (note 5)	(314)	(258)	(224)
Earnings	Earnings before income taxes and minority interest	2,493	2,391	2,153
	Provision for income taxes (note 6)	(958)	(953)	(894)
	Minority interest in earnings of consolidated affiliates	(21)	(29)	(29)
	Net earnings applicable to common stock	$ 1,514	$ 1,409	$ 1,230
	Earnings per common share (in dollars) (note 7)	$6.65	$6.20	$5.39
	Dividends declared per common share (in dollars)	$2.95	$2.75	$2.50
	Operating margin as a percentage of sales	9.0%	9.5%	10.0%
	Net earnings as a percentage of sales	6.1%	6.3%	6.3%

Statement of retained earnings

General Electric Company and consolidated affiliates

For the years ended December 31 (In millions)		1980	1979	1978
Retained earnings	Balance January 1	$6,307	$5,522	$4,862
	Net earnings	1,514	1,409	1,230
	Dividends declared on common stock	(670)	(624)	(570)
	Balance December 31	$7,151	$6,307	$5,522

Statement of financial position

General Electric Company and consolidated affiliates

At December 31 (In millions)		1980	1979
Assets	Cash (note 8)	$ 1,601	$ 1,904
	Marketable securities (note 8)	600	672
	Current receivables (note 9)	4,339	3,647
	Inventories (note 10)	3,343	3,161
	Current assets	9,883	9,384
	Property, plant and equipment – net (note 11)	5,780	4,613
	Investments (note 12)	1,820	1,691
	Other assets (note 13)	1,028	956
	Total assets	$18,511	$16,644
Liabilities and equity	Short-term borrowings (note 14)	$ 1,093	$ 871
	Accounts payable (note 15)	1,671	1,477
	Progress collections and price adjustments accrued	2,084	1,957
	Dividends payable	170	159
	Taxes accrued	628	655
	Other costs and expenses accrued (note 16)	1,946	1,753
	Current liabilities	7,592	6,872
	Long-term borrowings (note 17)	1,000	947
	Other liabilities	1,565	1,311
	Total liabilities	10,157	9,130
	Minority interest in equity of consolidated affiliates	154	152
	Preferred stock ($1 par value; 2,000,000 shares authorized; none issued)	—	—
	Common stock ($2.50 par value; 251,500,000 shares authorized; 231,463,949 shares issued 1980 and 1979)	579	579
	Amounts received for stock in excess of par value	659	656
	Retained earnings	7,151	6,307
		8,389	7,542
	Deduct common stock held in treasury	(189)	(180)
	Total share owners' equity (notes 18, 19, and 20)	8,200	7,362
	Total liabilities and equity	$18,511	$16,644
	Commitments and contingent liabilities (note 21)		

Statement of changes in financial position

General Electric Company and consolidated affiliates

For the years ended December 31 (In millions)		1980	1979	1978
Source of funds	From operations			
	Net earnings	$1,514	$1,409	$1,230
	Depreciation, depletion and amortization	707	624	576
	Investment tax credit deferred — net	56	45	25
	Income tax timing differences	63	(37)	32
	Earnings retained by nonconsolidated finance affiliates	(22)	(17)	(16)
	Minority interest in earnings of consolidated affiliates	21	29	29
		2,339	2,053	1,876
	Increase in long-term borrowings	122	50	96
	Newly issued common stock	—	—	3
	Disposition of treasury shares	136	148	190
	Increase in current payables other than short-term borrowings	498	786	570
	Decrease in investments	—	—	24
	Other — net	143	101	150
	Total source of funds	3,238	3,138	2,909
Application of funds	Additions to property, plant and equipment	1,948	1,262	1,055
	Dividends declared on common stock	670	624	570
	Increase in investments	129	281	—
	Reduction in long-term borrowings	69	97	386
	Purchase of treasury shares	145	156	196
	Increase in current receivables	692	358	306
	Increase in inventories	182	158	399
	Total application of funds	3,835	2,936	2,912
Net change	Net change in cash, marketable securities and short-term borrowings	$ (597)	$ 202	$ (3)
Analysis of net change	Increase (decrease) in cash and marketable securities	$ (375)	$ 113	$ 185
	Decrease (increase) in short-term borrowings	(222)	89	(188)
	Increase (decrease) in net liquid assets	$ (597)	$ 202	$ (3)

Index